OUSMANE SEMBÈNE

OUSMANE SEMBÈNE

Dialogues with Critics and Writers

edited by

SAMBA GADJIGO,

RALPH FAULKINGHAM,

THOMAS CASSIRER,

and

REINHARD SANDER

University of Massachusetts Press

Amherst

This book first appeared in October 1993 as a special issue of *Contributions in Black Studies*, published by the Five Colleges Black Studies Executive Committee with the support of Five Colleges, Inc.: Amherst, Hampshire, Mount Holyoke, and Smith Colleges and the University of Massachusetts.

This paperback edition is distributed by the
University of Massachusetts Press, Box 429, Amherst, MA 01004
413–545–2219
ISBN 0-87023-889-2
LC 93–8910

Frontispiece photo of Ousmane Sembène by Paul H. Schnaittacher

Library of Congress Cataloging-in-Publication Data
Ousmane Sembène : dialogues with critics and writers /
edited by Samba Gadjigo . . . [et al.].
p.   cm.
"First published in 1993 as a special issue of the journal
Contributions in Black studies"—Verso t.p.
English and French
Based primarily on a conference held in Amherst, Mass., in April 1990.
Includes bibliographical references and filmography.
ISBN 0–87023–889–2 (pbk.)
1. Sembène, Ousmane, 1923—Criticism and interpretation—Congresses
2. Motion pictures—Senegal—History—Congresses.
I. Gadjigo, Samba, 1954–
PN1998.3.S397088   1993
791.43'0233'092—dc20   93–8910
                                                    CIP

British Library Cataloguing in Publication data are available.

CONTENTS

PREFACE

At the invitation of the Five College African Studies Council and with funds provided by Five Colleges, Inc., the great Senegalese filmmaker and novelist Ousmane Sembène came to the five campuses for the first two weeks of April 1990. The dialectic of Sembène's own personal biography and the forms of his creative work framed a motif for a conference culminating his visit, appropriately titled "The Dialectics of Form and Content in the Works of Ousmane Sembène," held at the University of Massachusetts in Amherst on April 14. We planned the conference to be the high point of his stay, where those students and faculty who had attended Sembène's appearances and film screenings during the previous two weeks would have a chance to hear scholarly analyses of his work and to witness his dialogues with writers from Africa and the diaspora. Furthermore, the evening session of this one-day conference provided the opportunity to stage the North American premiere of Sembène's 1989 film, "Camp de Thiaroye."

The heart of this volume is based on that day's presentations and dialogues. While the conference was the high point of Sembène's residency, his entire visit came after a decade of organization and cooperation that gave rise to the Five College African Studies program. The program had begun in earnest in 1980 as a forum for faculty in the Five College area to share their interests in Africa. The guiding principles of our collaboration from the beginning were that it would be a collective enterprise, it would be multidisciplinary, and it would close the gulf between African Studies and African-American Studies. The Sembène visit and conference celebrated these principles.

The readiness of editor Ernest Allen to publish the Ousmane Sembène Conference in its entirety in *Contributions in Black Studies* underscores the recognition of similar, even common, experiences and cultural roots of Africans and those of the African diaspora. Making sense of these commonalities was the central theme of writers, critics, and questioners at the conference. For the generation after World War II, the interests, intellectual and political, of Africans and descendants of Africa in the diaspora, had been divided into distinct experiential and hermeneutic domains. On university campuses, African-American Studies had been legitimated within a context of the experience of African Americans in the Americas, while African Studies laid claim to the study of Africa itself emerging from colonial rule. This division of labor may have possessed a certain bureaucratic logic, but it had unfortunate cultural and political consequences. African-American Studies were divorced from African Studies; even the ethnic composition of those practicing in these two fields became noticeably distinct. Since the 1980s, however, we find in the academy a reconceptualization of African Studies and African-American Studies that has caught up with realities off-campus and affirmed a position W. E. B. Du Bois championed more than 75 years ago: the study of Africa and the African diaspora is a seamless whole.

It was Samba Gadjigo's idea to bring his compatriot to the Five Colleges, and knowing Sembène's general policy of refusing invitations to come to North America, Samba agreed to travel to Senegal to issue the invitation personally. What the rest of us took to be highly improbable—that Sembène would actually accept our invitation—Samba serenely assumed to be a *fait accompli*. Reinhard Sander was able to coax Ngugi wa Thiong'o, whom he befriended during his days at the University of Bayreuth, to come to the conference, along with Earl Lovelace and Toni Cade Bambara. Reinhard, chair of the Five College African Studies Council at the time, presided over the details of Sembène's visit. For Tom Cassirer and Ralph Faulkingham, the Sembène visit represented the culmination of a decade of work to organize the Africanists at each of the five campuses into a coherent and purposeful Five College African Studies program. Tom had been teaching Sembène's films and novels in his French courses for some time, and he luxuriated in the repartee with Sembène. For Sembène's visit, Ralph became the "exchequer," soliciting dollars from many quarters, reining in Samba's and Reinhard's budgetary ambitions, and organizing the details of the conference itself.

When it came to putting together this volume, we assumed different and complementary writing and editing roles. The preface, acknowledgments, introductions to Parts I and II, biographical notes on contributors, and the filmography were written by Ralph Faulkingham. The four of us shared the task of editing the critics' oral presentations into their final written form. Samba Gadjigo and Tom Cassirer went over the transcriptions and the original tapes of Sembène's remarks in order to establish an accurate text, then Tom Cassirer translated this text into English. Ralph Faulkingham and Reinhard Sander edited the transcriptions of the other writers' remarks, and Samba Gadjigo contributed both the annotated bibliography of Sembène's works as well as the bibliography of critical reviews of Sembène's writing and films. Finally, Ralph Faulkingham acted as the contact person with the editors at *Contributions in Black Studies* and at the University of Massachusetts Press. He also took on the job of integrating the disparate portions of the manuscript into a unified text. The final copy editing was our joint responsibility.

For the four of us, working together to bring Ousmane Sembène to the Five Colleges, organizing the Conference that this volume recounts, and finally editing the transcript of that day's events have cemented our friendship. Sembène's social and political critique of oppression—a critique intellectualized and written as well as

practiced in everyday life—his humanity and abundant good humor, and his optimism—that out of struggle will come a new distinctly African way of economic,
political, and cultural development—inspire us still.

On Sembène's first evening in the United States, as we were driving him back
to his dormitory room at Mount Holyoke College after dinner, he inquired: *"Qu'est-
ce que j'ai à dire aux étudiants? Je ne suis pas un académicien."* [What do I have to
say to the students? I'm not an academic.] Perhaps his question was prompted by jet
lag from his flight from Dakar or from anxiety as he anticipated his first extended stay
in an American academic community. Yet his query set the tone for the entire visit,
and against his own expectations, anticipated the extraordinary impact of his presence.

Rather than delivering lectures in the usual academic manner, Sembène engaged in a series of public conversations with audiences on all five campuses, usually
prompted by students' questions of him and his work. It was precisely the fact that
Sembène was one of the most "unacademic" writers, not only in Africa, but in the
entire world, that accounted for his instant rapport with students, faculty, and
eventually with a wider public of more than 500 people who attended the conference.
His passion for acquiring knowledge, his insistence on flouting convention when it
challenged principle, and his patient, often humorous, and thoughtful responses to
questions endeared him to us all.

Part One of this volume represents the morning session of the conference, with
the four essays by distinguished literary and film critics. At the conclusion of their
presentations, Sembène provides his own response. And characteristically, he refers
not to their discussion of him, but to the issues he develops in his work.

Part Two is based on the afternoon session, where Sembène and four other
widely known writers—Toni Cade Bambara, Earl Lovelace, Ngugi wa Thiong'o, and
John Wideman—discuss their craft.

Part Three represents Sembène's comments after a packed house of several
hundred people watched his film "Camp de Thiaroye." At the end of the afternoon
session, Sembène told us he was going back to his apartment for a nap. We did not
expect him to return in the evening to view his own film. But as the house lights went
up at the closing of the film, Sembène and his interpreter Kango Laré-Lantone strode
to the front of the auditorium to a standing ovation. His comments were unanticipated
and spontaneous.

Part Four contains an interview that Sada Niang of the University of Victoria
(British Columbia) conducted with Sembène on the occasion of his visit to Toronto
in July 1992. Professor Niang, after correspondence and telephone calls with Samba
Gadjigo, discussing possible topics for the interview, oriented his questions to
complement the April 1990 conference.

Following the biographical notes on the conference participants, the Appendix contains brief annotations of Sembène's written works and films as well as a select bibliography of critical works on Sembène.

Most of the text of this volume is in English; nonetheless, to preserve the character of Sembène's voice, his remarks are represented as he spoke them, in French. Throughout the volume French text is italicized, and it is followed immediately by a translation in English.

ACKNOWLEDGMENTS

We gratefully acknowledge the generous support that we received from many individuals, as we hosted Sembène's visit to the Five College area, in organizing the Ousmane Sembène conference, and in bringing this volume to publication. In particular, we want to single out several individuals for their specific contributions. Alison Friedman, having just returned for her senior year at Smith College from a visit to Senegal, managed both Sembène's office at Mount Holyoke College and his daily schedule while he was here; she used her good judgment and organizational skills to ensure that Sembène's visit was pleasant and productive for him and for the entire Five College community. Kango Laré-Lantone, completing a Ph.D. degree in economics at the University of Massachusetts, was pressed into service to interpret for Ousmane Sembène. Grateful for the opportunity to meet the author he had read while growing up in Togo, Kango worked tirelessly with skill and good humor, interpreting in both directions between French and English.

Catherine Portuges graciously agreed to moderate a panel at the conference after having highlighted Sembène's visit with a long article in the journal *Moving Images*, which she edits. John Montague of New Yorker Films expedited the development of a 16mm version of Sembène's film "Camp de Thiaroye" just in time for the conference. Deborah A. Salkaus of the University of Massachusetts Conference Services coordinated all the details of hosting the conference, while Sarah Faulkingham and Judy Kellogg took on the arduous task of transcribing the Conference proceedings, and did it admirably.

We had the luxury of the thoroughly professional and indefatigable support at the Five College Center from Jackie Pritzen, Carol Angus, Jean Stabell, and Gail Porter. E. Jefferson "Pat" Murphy as Five College Coordinator had prodded the Five College African Studies Council into existence a dozen years ago. His successor Conn Nugent had wisely chosen to fund the African Studies Council's proposal to bring Ousmane Sembène here for an extended visit, and Lorna Peterson, who in turn succeeded Conn Nugent, gave us her sage advice and frequent encouragement. The Five College African Studies Council, Black Studies Executive Committee, and Film Studies Council lent further financial backing to our project.

At Amherst College, we enjoyed the support of the Department of Black Studies, the English Department Language and Literature Fund, and the Office of the Dean of the Faculty.

On the Hampshire College campus, the Office of the Dean of the Faculty and the Office of the Dean of Multicultural Affairs helped out, while at Mount Holyoke

College, the Department of French arranged a seminar for Sembène, President Elizabeth Kennan hosted a reception at her home to honor Sembène, and the Office of the Dean of Faculty provided a suite of rooms for Sembène to live in for the duration of his visit.

At Smith College, the Sembène conference was supported by the Office of the Dean of the Faculty, while at the University of Massachusetts at Amherst, we received grants from the Dean of the Faculty of Humanities and Fine Arts, the Department of Anthropology, the Institute for Advanced Study in the Humanities, and the Office of International Programs.

Finally, we want to thank the many hundreds of students, faculty, and visitors who attended the screenings of Sembène's films and his public discussions, as well as the conference itself. Their interest, engagement, and provocative questions were crucial to the success of Sembène's visit and to his evident pleasure in being here.

PART ONE

CRITICAL PERSPECTIVES ON THE WORKS OF OUSMANE SEMBÈNE

In response to a student's question about his background, Ousmane Sembène recalled that he had been expelled from primary school in Senegal for striking back at his French teacher who had slapped him. His fisherman father was not particularly perturbed by this cataclysmic event—cataclysmic because it closed the school door permanently for Sembène. In fact, he was pleased with his son's strident defense of his invaded personhood.

In time, through his own self-education, Sembène appropriated the forms of the colonizing French culture—reading, speaking, and writing its language. And he gained a fluency in understanding its representations and what the French called their *mission civilisatrice* in Africa in order to accomplish in his life what his school boy reaction foreshadowed: to reclaim from colonial and neocolonial misrepresentation the reality of an African past and present and to proclaim the dignity, independence, and power of African cultural forms for the continent's future.

As Fred Case's essay in this section notes, Sembène readily represents himself as a griot, evoking the West African personage of ambiguous social placement who faithfully recounts the traditions of the past while providing a pointed critique of the present. Sembène's novels and films represent a griot's extended commentary on African realities, not the myths of Africa invented by Africans or Europeans. Unlike so many of his literary peers on the continent who received the best education colonial systems could offer, Sembène is a supreme example of a successful writer who is self-educated—he was a soldier and a dock worker before turning to writing. Then in his late thirties, largely for the practical reason of wanting to reach a non-literate African audience, Sembène turned to film. And again, unlike his peers in francophone Africa, he went not to France but to the Gorki Institute in Moscow for his technical training in filmmaking. Sembène's own experience may explain why his work does not conjure up the simplicity of the African village, but instead often focuses on industrial and urban settings, examining the character and motives of those who seek to exploit the changed social conditions of the post-colonial economy and polity in modern West Africa. His films and novels now, at the end of the twentieth century, are gaining a

1

widening audience and international critical acclaim far beyond the shores of Africa.

Because the language of Sembène's work is French, Wolof, or Diola, his novels and films are not as widely known in the anglophone world as they should be, although by the end of the 1980s, nearly all of his writing had been translated into English. Neither have his works—until fairly recently—been part of the francophone canon, perhaps for reasons of his class, education, and political orientation. Nonetheless, writers and filmmakers in Africa and throughout the African diaspora readily acknowledge his influence on their own artistry and his pre-eminence as the founder of African cinema and as one of Africa's great writers.

A pervasive characteristic of Sembène's work is the treatment of Africa in terms of itself, without a preconditional Europe. This is not to assert that Sembène is artistically unaware of the crucial roles played by Europe or by Islam in shaping the forms of modern Africa's political economy and society. He is quite cognizant of these; indeed, he shows how they have contributed to contemporary African realities. Yet he insists that Africans occupy the center of his stage, that their humanity—as the oppressed and the oppressors—be understood for what it is. He films and writes for an African audience, not a European or American one. Of his regular practice of showing his films to Senegalese peasants, he once said: *"Le cinéma est l'école du soir du peuple."* [The cinema is the people's night school.] As a teacher and as a griot Sembène wants his films to remind, to instruct, and to provoke his viewers. In Senegal, his unrelenting social criticism has put him continually at odds with those in political, economic, or religious power.

The essays in this section provide various critical glimpses of Sembène's creative work. The first, by Fred Case, traces the linguistic and semantic devices Sembène deploys in his written work to represent his own social and ideological commitments. Mbye Cham's discussion, on the other hand, examines how Sembène in his films and in his writing contrasts both dominant and subordinate representations of the African past. The essay by Françoise Pfaff traces the social themes that mark Sembène's films, while the concluding essay by Claire Andrade-Watkins lays bare the historical, political, and cultural conditions under which Sembène's films were produced.

Aesthetics, Ideology, and Social Commitment in the Prose Fiction of Ousmane Sembène

by Frederick Ivor Case

NEW COLLEGE
UNIVERSITY OF TORONTO

The prose fiction of Ousmane Sembène[1] is very easy to comprehend on the surface but it is, in fact, profoundly complex. There is a remarkable consistency in his work: a preoccupation with the struggles of the working poor and the unemployed; and also with the exploitation and oppression of a relentless capitalism that seriously threatens the social and cultural structures of society as well as the inner recesses of the mind. There is also a consistent aesthetic context in his work, in which African artistic principles underlie and undermine the limitations of French forms of expression, since these forms do not always provide the author with the semantic, linguistic, and symbolic tools he needs. In *L'Harmattan*, Ousmane Sembène writes a brief foreword to the reader, a relatively rare phenomenon for this author:

> *Je ne fais pas la théorie du roman africain. Je me souviens pourtant que jadis, dans cette Afrique qui passe pour classique, le griot était non seulement l'élément dynamique de sa tribu, clan, village, mais aussi le témoin patent de chaque événement. C'est lui qui enregistrait, déposait devant tous, sous l'arbre du palabre, les faits et gestes de chacun. La conception de mon travail découle de cet enseignement: rester au plus près du réel et du peuple. (p. 9)*

> [I do not intend to produce a theory of the African novel. I remember, however, that long ago, in that Africa that is revered, the griot was not only the dynamic element of his tribe, clan, and village, but also the authentic witness of each event. It is he who recorded and deposited before us, under the tree, the deeds and exploits of each person. The conception of my work is derived from this teaching: to remain as close as possible to reality and to the people.]

It is important to consider this declaration since it clearly indicates that Ousmane Sembène's realism is derived directly from an African vision of literature. However, in so far as this vision of literary expression is intimately associated with the interpretation of the lives of individuals and their relationship to their social context it is also an ideological statement. One can say that there are several recurring themes in Sembène's work and that his ideological thought includes consideration of various aspects of the human condition.

However, the major ideological principle that characterizes his work is the recognition of the rights of women in society and the affirmation of their economic, social, and cultural role in the dynamic determination of the destinies of African peoples.[2] I emphasize the plural of women since Sembène's work is devoid of the individualistic love-marriage, or love-triangle focus which makes up the vast body of western prose fiction.[3] There *is* individual action by Sembène's female protagonists but this type of action has to be seen within the context of the isolation often imposed on them through marriage. In this way, even their individual acts of revolt are not individualistic and divisive but are actions that tend toward the healing of specific ills in society. Sembène has therefore chosen to produce his work within the specific cultural norms of African society, which tends to live out its tensions and conflicts on a family, community, or collective basis.

It is no coincidence that Sembène's prose fiction shares the characteristics of a great diversity of African writers. It has the aesthetic and ontological depth and versatility of Bessie Head's *A Question of Power*;[4] the deeply rooted commitment to the working poor of Ngugi wa Thiong'o's *A Grain of Wheat*;[5] the courageous defiance of Nawal El Saadawi's *The Hidden Face of Eve*;[6] the religious cynicism of Driss Chraïbi's *Le passé simple*[7] and Assia Djebar's *Les femmes d'Alger dans leur appartement*;[8] and the very precise aesthetic elements of African literary expression we find in Achebe's *Things Fall Apart*.[9]

In a recently completed work, "Poétique linguistique de la littérature sénégalaise: Une analyse diachronique,"[10] Sada Niang details the semantic and linguistic evolution in the works of Ousmane Sembène. Niang identifies four linguistic stages in the evolution of Sembène's prose. The first stage spans the period 1956 to 1960 with the publication of *Le docker noir, O pays, mon beau peuple*, and *Les bouts de bois de Dieu*. Niang writes of this period:

> *De la première à la troisième et en très peu de temps nous passons d'une utilisation indifférenciée et quasi mythique du registre standard de la langue française à une contextualisation partielle de ce registre puis enfin à un usage qui pose l'existence d'un sous texte wolof au niveau de la narration tout aussi bien que celui des dialogues.* (Niang, p. 68)

> [From the first work to the third, in a short period of time, we progress from a consistent and almost mythical use of standard French to a partial contextualisation of this register and finally to a means of expression which produces a Wolof sub-text in the narration as well as in the dialogues.]

Thus by the time that Ousmane Sembène wrote his second novel, published in 1957, he had begun to transform the French language primarily through the dialogues. In this novel *O pays, mon beau peuple* a group of men gather before the time of prayer:

> *Tous les notables de la Croyance étaient là.*
> Avez-vous passé l'après-midi en paix?
> Paix seulement, répondait l'assemblée, et la famille?
> En paix, et vos familles?
> En paix, disaient les gens.
> *Que la paix augmente en ce saint lieu, dit Moussa en s'accroupissant.* (pp. 16-17)

> [All the notable personages of the Faith were there.
> "Have you passed the afternoon in peace?"
> "In peace only," replied the assembly, "and your family?"
> "In peace, and your families?"
> "In peace," said the others.
> "May peace grow in this holy place," said Moussa as he squatted.]

The use of the word "Croyance" (Faith), with a capital letter, emphasizes the importance of the assembly but also immediately creates a social context that is culturally appropriate. The men have gathered just before the time of prayer and are about to discuss an important matter. The greetings used are translated directly from Wolof and do not in any way correspond to greetings used in standard metropolitan French. From this point onwards Sembène's characters normally greet one another according to the cultural norms of their society. Deviation from this pattern is usually indicative of the degree of assimilation and alienation of a particular character. Hence in the short story "Taaw," published in 1987, the group of young men greet one another in a particular slang—a form of pidgin consisting of Wolof, French, and English:

> -Ey! Boy! Comment? Vous êtes tombés du lit? s'exclama Taaw. . .
> *-Non!. . .Non!. . .Boy. Nous sommes tombés de la natte, répliqua Mam Ass, faisant de l'esprit.* (pp. 69-73)

> ["Hey, man! What! Did you fall off your bed?" exclaimed Taaw. . .
> "No!. . .No. . .man. We fell off the mat," replied Mam Ass, jokingly.]

This new language of the young, unemployed men is indicative of the ideological and cultural distance that they have travelled from their fathers against whom the young men are in a state of open revolt. It could also be said that the frequent use of "Boy" and other expressions in English signals the extent to which this particular language register has evolved in terms of North American usage. The normal cultural greetings built around the notion of "peace" have become entirely hypocritical, empty formulas which maintain their beauty only for those who do not see or do not wish to see the fundamental contradictions between the discourse and its connotations. In the daily realities of the young men of "Taaw" there is no peace, nor is there harmony, but only hunger, unemployment, family conflict, and humiliation.

However, it is in *Les bouts de bois de Dieu* that we witness the mastery of semantic and linguistic devices that has produced a distinctive cultural vision in Ousmane Sembène's work. For many of us this great novel remains his masterpiece, and we look forward to the day when he will produce a film version of this great African epic.

I already pointed out several years ago, in an article,[11] that Penda is the main protagonist of this novel. During the march from Thies to Dakar, the wives and daughters of the striking railroad men reach a crisis situation (pp. 298-302). Penda is leading the march, but the seriously alienated Awa, who defines herself as the "wife of the foreman Sène Massène," attempts to gather some of the women around her in revolt. In the three pages that it takes Sembène to describe this particular incident we have three distinct semantic registers. Firstly, we have the standard international French of the protagonist Penda and the women who are ideologically close to her. This standard international French represents, in the text, the use of standard Wolof as a means of communication. This is a discourse that is firm but persuasive. It is a semanticism of positive cooperation but which, in an unambiguous manner, estab-lishes Penda as leader.

Secondly, we have the orders addressed to the men. This is a significant socio-linguistic phenomenon since in the long march between the industrial town and the capital city Penda gives only commands to the men she encounters. For example, she says to the small group of men who are accompanying the women:

> *Il faut qu'elles marchent. Vous, avec vos bidons, allez en tête et ne donnez à boire qu'à celles qui sont arrivées aux arbres, là-bas. Et toi, amène-moi près des autres.* (p. 299)

> [The women must continue walking. You men with your water cans, go ahead and give to drink only to those who arrive at the trees over there. And you, take me to the others.]

Four imperatives, four orders in three short sentences addressed to a group of men under her direct command. The rapid succession of verbs in the imperative form and the rapid succession of pronouns underline the superior/inferior relationship. Symbolically, Penda wears a military belt around her waist and this item of clothing emphasizes her position of authority. This is a new female discourse that announces the birth of a new gender relationship. This is not the voice of pleading but the assurance and security of a woman who is aware of her importance, her duties, and her responsibilities in her society. The men are forced to accept her command and some of the women find it difficult to adjust to this new situation.

Thirdly, in Penda's words to Awa and the other women in revolt, the semantic elements of the discourse are characterized by a refusal to respond directly to Awa's cruel taunts. Awa's mixture of Wolof and French bears only a surface meaning that is destructive and unsettling in its intention to manipulate. This very unstructured and individualistic language register, which is neither Wolof nor French nor a recognizable pidgin based on the two languages, aptly reflects the social and cultural alienation of this character who is used as a foil to Penda's characterization. Finally, Penda uses a method of rallying the women that seems, on the surface, to have nothing at all to do with the circumstances. By counting the women she uses a deeply held fear of enumeration to stir them all.[12] The belief system of the women goes far beyond Islam to a realm of consciousness in which indigenous religion and culture reign. Without replying to their protests she continues relentlessly counting—using the deep connotations of this enunciation which transforms a seemingly innocent exercise in the French language into a very threatening discourse in Wolof that is evocative of witchcraft. But this discourse is destined to achieve a particular social aim which is crystallized in the paragraph that closes this incident:

> *La colère et la crainte se partageant leur coeur, les femmes rassemblèrent leurs pagnes, ajustèrent leurs mouchoirs de tête, rejoignirent la route et reprirent la marche. A quelque distance les hommes suivaient, menés par Boubacar.* (p. 302)

> [Anger and fear tearing at their hearts the women took up their pagnes, adjusted their head scarves, went back on to the road and began to march again. A little distance away the men followed, led by Boubacar.]

The intensive usage of the *passé simple* in French emphasizes the rapid succession of actions as they continue on the march with the men following them. It is as though Sembène is telling us that it is only women who can organize themselves to undertake their own struggle against oppression. Sympathetic men will have no alternative but to follow and serve.

We learn in this same novel that one of the men had molested Penda while she was in the union building. She slapped him publicly, thereby asserting herself and demanding respect from all of the men.[13] To their sexual violence she replied immediately with violence, humiliating her assailant and asserting her right to appear anywhere without being molested.

Once again I refer to the short story "Taaw" because it is in this work that a mother—Yaye Dabo—revolts against her subjection to the will and arbitrary behavior of her husband. She is often brutalized by her husband and witnesses the repeated beatings administered to her children. Her husband is truly an odious man. In this case it is not polygamy as such that is criticized, as it is ridiculed in *Xala*, it is the assumption of male superiority and the pretensions to despotic male authority that lead Yaye Dabo to assert her rights in a most dramatic and meaningful manner. In her revolt she pushes her husband roughly to the ground, publicly repudiates and humiliates him "before witnesses" as she says, and forbids him to return to her home.[14] In an individual manner she has reversed the order of things in her world and has set an example before the other women and her own children.

It is very significant that twenty years before the completion of "Taaw" Ousmane Sembène completed that masterpiece of short stories, "Véhi-Ciosane." In this earlier short story the mother, Ngoné War Thiandum, kills herself because she cannot face the shame and dishonor created by the incest committed by her husband and her daughter. The father is eventually killed by their son while the women of the village succeed in expelling the young daughter from the community. In this short story, the women appear to have only very slight glimmers of consciousness of their situation, and this is perfectly understandable if one takes into account the geographic isolation and religious, cultural, and ethnic homogeneity of Santhiu-Niaye. The significant difference in "Taaw" is that the social dislocation of urbanization has, of itself, been an education for women. However, in "Véhi-Ciosane" it is one of the fathers in the community who poses the general problem of older men preying on adolescent girls. This enlightened father says to his peers:

> *Une fille de même âge que ta fille, une fille qui s'est amusée chez toi avec ta fille, que tu appelais hier, "mon enfant," une fille dont les parents disaient: "Va dire à ton père un tel," une fille que tu as baptisée, cette fille, en l'épousant, c'est ta fille que tu épouses, finit de dire Déthyè Law fixant l'imam avec défi. . .*(p. 70)

> ["A girl the same age as your daughter, a girl who has played with your daughter in your house; whom yesterday you called 'my child'; a girl whose parents said: 'Go and tell your father. . .'; a girl whom you named; if you marry her, you are marrying your daughter," said Déthyè Law staring at the imam in defiance.]

It is significant that this appears to be one of the least studied of Sembène's works. The subject of incest and adolescent brides of grandfathers is too delicate a subject for most intellectuals. Though the subject of marriage through duress is one of the major themes in *Xala*, its treatment is not as stark and tormenting as in "Véhi-Ciosane." Of course, as we know, incest is a forbidden topic of discussion in many societies and as a result of dealing with this question the Egyptian writer Nawal El Saadawi was imprisoned.[15] This abuse of the body of young children, and most frequently of young female children, when placed in the context of the infringement of human rights, of religious precepts and paternal authority, is not a subject that many wish to discuss because it is truly a universal situation of sexual exploitation that produces reactions of shame and disgust and that no human community wishes to face with frankness and honesty. For this reason it is the other short story in the volume *Le mandat* that is widely studied and commented on. Academics generally justify their refusal to study "Véhi-Ciosane" by referring to alleged inadequacies of style and structure which they can never specifically identify.

It is very rare that a male character of Sembène's work gives voice to the pain and suffering of women. But in "Véhi-Ciosane" it is the role of the one enlightened man of the community to educate the other men, and Déthyè Law's discourse concerning incest is addressed to his friends of Santhiu-Niaye as much as it is to the readers.

Sembène uses the male characters of his novels and short stories primarily to convey certain symbolic messages through their clothing, their gestures or the social context. The characterization of Bakayoko, the male protagonist of *Les bouts de bois de Dieu*, is a brilliant illustration of this depiction of a male character who despite his positive attributes is intellectually and socially incapable of undertaking the struggle on behalf of the women. He is the leader of the men who, through their atavism, have to have a clearly identifiable single male voice to galvanize them to action. Herd-like creatures through their socialization, men appear to be incapable of meaningful social and economic revolt. The railroad workers who follow Bakayoko win a few concessions from the company but nothing has changed in their relationship with one another and with their bosses. On the other hand, after Penda's death and the return of the women to Thies, the mothers, wives, and daughters of the railroad workers have significantly altered their relationships with one another, with their men folk and even with the company. This, surely, is the final test of meaningful change in society that women are capable of the positive transformation of gender relationships through the consciousness-raising process of revolt.

Throughout his prose fiction it is very clear that it is primarily through the discourse on and of his female characters that Sembène's ideological messages are conveyed. The narrative discourse of the text gives us a very clear indication of Sembène's perspectives on the condition of women. From the descriptions of the comfortable, wealthy old woman Djia Umbrel (*Le dernier de l'Empire*, p. 125) reading a book on African women written by an African woman, to the three wives of El Hadji Abdou Kader Bèye in *Xala* and the poor women of *Les bouts de bois de Dieu* and "Taaw," we obtain a consistent vision of oppression and of a growing revolt against subjugation.

But despite the examples of courageous revolt against exploitation contrasted with the negative words and actions of the alienated, Sembène's work also expresses a great optimism as far as individual human beings are concerned. One has only to think of the reversal of Awa's attitude and behavior toward the end of *Les bouts de bois de Dieu* and the birth of consciousness of the aged Cheikh Tidiane Fall in *Le dernier de l'Empire*. The ideological recuperation of characters who are initially drawn in a negative fashion points to an aesthetic that transcends mere social realism and that has a very clear didactic purpose.

In this context it is important to realize that Sembène's work does not dwell on the voluntary or involuntary submission of the women to their sexually, economically, psychologically, and socially inferior state. Even though in *Le dernier de l'Empire* (Vol. 1, pp. 94-98) we see a female secretary as the plaything of a minister, this is an incident of social importance rather than a theme. Such incidents are not gratuitous but lead to the central ideological theme of the work. Invariably, as in "Taaw," the oppression that is analyzed is a prelude to a significant revolt, but the abuse of male power has to be underlined in order to emphasize the degree to which husbands and fathers have become quite depraved individuals deeply in love with themselves and very protective of their outrageous privileges.

Perhaps the most outrageous but most significantly symbolic scene in all of Sembène's work is the moment in "Taaw"[16] when Goor Yummbul forces his pregnant daughter, Astou, to swallow her own vomit. But such scenes of extreme cruelty are infrequent in Sembène's work and his portrayal of the subjugation of women serves to prepare us for the revolt against such oppression. At times Sembène gives us only examples of frustrated aspirations and thwarted hopes of liberation but they are nevertheless hopes that provide evidence of a deep consciousness and the potential for change.

In "Lettres de France"[17] we read the inner thoughts of a young Senegalese woman as she writes to her female friend:

> *Te souviens-tu de nos rêves? de nos ambitions de jeunes filles? Nous voulions être affranchies de la tutelle d'un mari; être nos propres maîtresses, acheter ce que nous voulions, sans avoir à s'expliquer, ou à attendre qu'une tierce personne nous donne de quoi nous le payer: en somme être libres.*

> [Do you remember our dreams, our ambitions when we were young? We wished to be free of the tutelage of a husband; to be mistresses of our own destiny; to buy whatever we wished without having to give explanations to anyone or without having to wait for someone else to give us money. In short we wished to be free.]

In her letter Ta Nafi expresses the women's struggle primarily in personal economic terms, and this is indeed a major trait of Sembène's female characters: they envisage freedom primarily as freedom from economic dependence. Ta Nafi is married to an elderly, unemployed man in Marseille. She is practically imprisoned in the unhealthy atmosphere of their one room that seems to re-create, in France, the culture of Senegal and to render the social and psychological stifling of the woman doubly burdensome.

Ramatoulaye, in *Les bouts de bois de Dieu*, and Yaye Dabo, in "Taaw," have also taken very practical economic steps to alter their condition. In *Les bouts de bois de Dieu* the march led by the female protagonist, Penda, leads to a liberty of action that the women had never known before. Their consciousness of their strength and their ability to effect change in society result in a militancy that has the potential of setting the entire society in motion. In "Taaw," where the immediate results of Yaye Dabo's dramatic revolt appear to outweigh the long-term consequences, her actions are presented within the following context:

> . . .*La famine, la sécheresse ne poussent pas seulement les familles à l'exode, elles détruisent, disloquent la communauté, brisent l'unité familiale. L'urbanisme, l'expansion du centre commercial poussent les mal lotis vers le faubourg. Et ici, parmi nous, nous avons des pauvres misérables. Demain c'est de ces faubourgs que naîtront le chef ou les chefs, les vrais.* (p. 170)

> [. . .Famine and drought do more than compel families to leave. They destroy, dislocate the community and break up family unity. Urbanization, the expansion of the commercial center push the have-nots toward the suburbs. And here among us we have poor miserable people. Tomorrow it is from these suburbs that the true leader or leaders will be born.]

Aminata, the woman who pronounces these words, is very unorthodox in her manners; she does not portray the submissiveness of the other women and is well known for her invective. In a very subjective way she resembles Penda. Indeed, Aminata's words recall Fanon's theory that it is the urban poor of Africa who will lead the revolt against the alienating structures of society.[18] The vision is no longer merely prophetic since we already see the results of the frustrations and aspirations of the young, urban poor of that continent. In *Le dernier de l'Empire* (Vol. 2, pp. 57-61) one sees very clearly that the struggle of the Senegalese people has to be conceived within the context of the universal struggle of oppressed peoples. But in this case it is the narrative discourse that provides us with these elements.

Similarly, in "Le mandat" and "Niiwam" it is more the narrative discourse than the dialogues which describes the abject helplessness of the two male protagonists faced with a bureaucratic state apparatus that they do not understand. In many ways "Niiwam," completed in 1977, is much more powerful than "Le mandat" published in 1966. In "Niiwam," Thierno and his wife arrive in Dakar with their ailing son. The very night of their arrival their son dies on the floor of the hospital and the father has to bury him. As the morgue is full, the father is given the necessary papers with great speed and relief, and he sets out with the little body covered in cloth to catch a bus to the cemetery. Niiwam is the name of the child and the title of the short story which is the tale of the journey to the cemetery. Sembène constantly draws the contrast between relationships in Thierno's home village and Dakar; between death and burial in the village and this undignified almost anonymous happening in Dakar. Very much as we have seen in "Le mandat," the relentless tyranny of the economic order, the frenzied pace of an unadapted technology and the totally dehumanizing bureaucratic structure deprive the individual of any hope of determining his present or future. This is a general situation that engulfs the entire population. The juxtaposition of positive, traditional modes of life and the struggle against dehumanizing technology and urbanization bring out many aspects of the creation of peripheries by international capitalism. Sembène's social analyses are most often implicit in the text. He does not indulge in writing political pamphlets but there is no uncertainty concerning the specific political orientation of his work.

Ousmane Sembène's use of the French language, which he has forced to its semantic limits by producing a new polysemy that is primarily Wolof; his acknowledgement of the primacy of indigenous culture and Islam as the motivating forces of the modes of thought of a people; his commitment to change and his consistent ideological discourse are the textual, literary evidence of a determined revolutionary purpose.

I have the impression, on the basis of a major study in which I am currently engaged, that the exercise of writing in French, that is, the process of concretizing in written form a number of social concepts and realities observed and experienced in an entirely different semantic, syntactic and symbolic framework, leads to a most intimate knowledge of the aesthetic demands placed on an author who seeks to articulate the aspirations of a people. This explains why the films made on the basis of the published works are even more powerful social statements than the written texts. It is not simply that the visual qualities of the cinema are used to impress us. I would like to suggest that in the particular case of Ousmane Sembène, the aesthetic quality of the film, its psychological and social impact, its lucid ideological discourse are the direct result of the struggle with questions of articulation and the need to bring to the written text a degree of limpidity that permits the intricacies of a multiplicity of contradictions to be expressed.

This is the genius of Ousmane Sembène, that his vision and his work are the expression of his ideology; that his films in Wolof or other African languages are presented in a semantic and symbolic language that conveys several aspects of the same message at one and the same time.

In the field of discourse analysis a distinction is made between the *énoncé* (that which is enunciated) and the *énonciation* (the process of enunciation). Ousmane Sembène has mastered the art of manipulating the process of enunciation in order to convey his message succinctly but in detail. He has mastered the intellectual feat of expressing Wolof concepts and semantic patterns in a language that appears at first to be ill-suited to such cultural enrichment. His serious themes and particular linguistic devices are the negation of the exoticism that a certain audience seeks in African works. His writing is a most careful, studied, and determined enterprise in which his stylistic versatility has been a consistent element.

Ousmane Sembène has achieved his literary success not in order to win prestigious literary prizes but to provide a social and political service to African peoples wherever they may be found. Though his prose fiction is in French he has provided us with a monument to African cultural expression and has demonstrated that, without compromise, and without adhering to some mystical ethos of the French language, this language can be transformed to serve the needs of African peoples as is true of even the most banal means of communication.

I cannot conclude these remarks without reiterating the most important lesson of Sembène's work: It is only through the positive transformation of gender relations, the acknowledgement and respect of the human rights of women, their affirmation and seizing of their economic and social rights, that meaningful, revolutionary change will be engendered in society. When the history of African feminist thought of the late twentieth century is written, a significant chapter should be devoted to the work of Ousmane Sembène.

The Uniqueness of Ousmane Sembène's Cinema

by Françoise Pfaff

HOWARD UNIVERSITY

The author of two documentary and nine fiction films made over a period of twenty-five years, Ousmane Sembène is presently one of Africa's leading writers as well as the continent's best-known film director. His seminal films, by their very nature, content, and style, have left an indelible mark on the history of African filmmaking. Before launching his career as a writer and filmmaker, Sembène had worked as a mason, carpenter, mechanic, dock worker, union organizer, and had also served as a sharpshooter in the French colonial army during the Second World War.

Many critics agree that the major characteristic of Sembène's career as a writer and a filmmaker is his socio-political commitment. And here we have to remember that it was precisely his concern to reach out to the largely non-literate African masses, his empathy with Senegal's common people, which led him to embrace a film career. Ousmane Sembène, who came in contact with Soviet socialist realism while studying film in Moscow, does not make films to entertain his compatriots, but rather to raise their awareness as to the past and present realities of their society. He once stated in an interview:

> What interests me is exposing the problems confronting my people. I consider the cinema to be a means for political action. Nevertheless I don't want to make "poster films." Revolutionary films are another thing. Moreover, I am not so naïve as to think that I could change Senegalese reality with a single film. But I think that if there were a whole group of us making films with that same orientation, we could alter reality a little bit.[19]

The originality of Ousmane Sembène as a filmmaker lies in his having managed successfully to adapt film, a primarily Western medium, to the needs, pace, and rhythm of African culture. And indeed, Sembène has found within his own culture the essence and strategies which allow him to express himself and to reach out effectively to both literate and non-literate Senegalese viewers. He has done so by way of their pre-literate tradition embodied in the timeless West African tradition of the griot with whom Sembène frequently identifies. In 1978, in the course of an interview, Sembène told me:

> The African filmmaker is like the griot who is similar to the European medieval minstrel: a man of learning and common sense who is the historian, the raconteur, the living memory and the conscience of his people. The filmmaker must live within his society and say what goes wrong within his society. Why does the filmmaker have such a role? Because like many other artists, he is maybe more sensitive than other people. Artists know the magic of words, sounds, and colors and they use these elements to illustrate what others think and feel. The filmmaker must not live secluded in an ivory tower; he has a definite social function to fulfill.[20]

Sembène's adherence to the African oral tradition has greatly influenced his cinematic output, which is frequently adapted from his written works. It is as a griot— and within a moralistic and didactic framework—that Sembène tackles with ease a multiplicity of topics, many of which are related to his own life experiences. It is as an attentive and concerned griot that Sembène interprets the socio-historical and cultural heritage of his community. His depictions are equally forceful whether he narrates the frustrating day of a Dakar cart-man ("Borom Sarret," 1963), or the tragic fate of a Senegalese maid in France who commits suicide ("Black Girl," 1966). Moreover, the filmmaker's familiarity with both the rural and urban settings of his country[21] allows him to describe with great insight and feeling the story of incest which actually took place in a Senegalese village in colonial times ("Niaye," 1964), as well as the fate of a young unemployed youth in Dakar ("Taaw," 1970). Further, Sembène's knowledge of the conflicts and contradictions found within a developing nation also inspired him to write and film "Mandabi" (1968), whose plot illustrates the tribulations and bitterness of a non-literate middle-aged man confronted with the complexities of modern bureaucracy. For the Senegalese director, it appears that art should neither hide nor embellish reality. Therefore, Sembène does not avoid sensitive issues such as polygamy, nepotism, and corruption, described in both "Mandabi" and "Xala." "Xala," made in 1975, is a biting satire about the economic impotence of Senegal's post-colonial elite. His most recent work, "Gelwaar" (1992), denounces foreign aid, religious intolerance, and bureaucratic red tape in a contemporary Senegalese setting.

Besides chronicling life in a contemporary setting, the traditional African griot is also a historian who reconstructs the legendary deeds of past heroes to whom he attributes contemporary moral significance. As such, Sembène incorporates in his thematic scope important events in African history which have often been forgotten or neglected in the Western historical canon. His very first film "L'Empire Sonhrai" (1963), which has never been distributed internationally, describes the historical importance of the city of Timbuktu and the Songhai resistance to French colonialism. Furthermore, Sembène's unshakable faith in the teachings of history and his progressive belief that African women have a major role to play in the evolution of society are strongly presented in "Emitaï" (1971). This motion picture depicts the rebellion of a village, spearheaded by the women who collectively protest France's increasing demands for recruits and rice from its overseas colonies in the early 1940s. A subsequent work, "Ceddo" (1976), scrutinizes in an allegorical style the various forces (traditional rule, Islam and European mercantilism) which were present in Senegal at the time of the slave trade. Through this study of political and religious expansion, the audience comes to question the authoritative structures which permitted (and in some instances invited) foreign powers to penetrate the African continent. "Ceddo" was prohibited from being publicly screened for eight years in Senegal, a fact which attests to the film's disquieting content and to Sembène's unflinching integrity and courage as he unveils political and historical truths, uncomfortable to those in power. This is especially noteworthy considering the fact that his earlier films "Xala" and "Emitaï" had already been censored before they could be released in Senegal.

Sembène's recent film, "Camp de Thiaroye" (1989), which received the highest award at the Venice Film Festival, was co-directed with the Senegalese filmmaker Thierno Faty Sow. Here, the former artillery soldier excavates and re-evaluates once more events which took place during the Second World War: the odious killing by the French army of African infantrymen who had rebelled against unfair treatment after having fought alongside the French troops in Europe. Since 1982, the director has been actively working on "Samori," a high-budget historical epic, envisioned as both a film and a television series. This project focuses on Samori Touré, a famous nineteenth-century leader of the resistance against French colonial imperialism in West Africa.

Sembène not only defines himself as a griot, he also includes this character in a number of his cinematic works. The griot is shown performing various functions as the actor/narrator of "Niaye" and the cart driver's family griot in "Borom Sarret." In "Xala," griots are also part of a celebration following the "Senegalization" of the Chamber of Commerce and the wedding festivities of the protagonist, El Hadji. In "Ceddo," Fara, a griot, follows the princess and her captor, and one can imagine that it is through him as well as through the griot-filmmaker that their story has been transmitted to us. "Ceddo" also included Jaraaf, a court griot who praises the merits of noblemen and serves as an intermediary between the king and his subjects, thus informing us of the protocol followed in the courts of ancient West African kingdoms.

A number of Sembène's characters can be associated with those found in traditional African storytelling. Many African oral stories contain the king and the princess, legendary forebears known to all. These characters are featured in Sembène's films as well. The trickster, for instance, usually a dishonest individual who personifies antisocial traits, appears as the thief or the corrupted civil servant or a member of an elite in "Borom Sarret," "Mandabi," and "Xala." The beggars and physically deformed people who are often part of African tales are present in such films as

"Borom Sarret" and "Xala." In "Xala," the jealous co-wife Oumi and the naïve peasant, who gets robbed as he comes to town, are stock characters of West African folklore. The tree which figures in countless African tales and which symbolizes knowledge, life, death, and rebirth or the link between heaven and earth is omnipresent in "Emitaï." Most of Sembène's characters are types reflecting collective ideas and attitudes. In oral African narratives, these types respond to typical situations, and so does the protagonist of "Borom Sarret," who has no name and is remembered through his trade and the problems he is unable to overcome. The heroine of "Black Girl" has universal facets: she is the victimized maid rather than Diouanna. "Mandabi's" principal character is the non-literate traditionalist rather than Ibrahima Dieng. "Xala's" El Hadji Abdou Kader Bèye is perceived as the unscrupulous impotent businessman, and "Ceddo's" female protagonist remains as the princess in the minds of film viewers.

Thematic similarities can also be drawn from a comparison between Sembène's films and African tales. Male impotence, which constitutes the basis of "Xala," is in itself a subject which is often included in the storyteller's repertoire. "Xala's" theme of punishment of greed, selfishness, vanity, and waste is likewise highly popular in African folktales, and so are topics of the lowly rebelling against the powerful. Moreover, Sembène's motion pictures derive from African dilemma tales, the outcome of which is debated and in a way decided by the spectators. With the open-endedness of most of his plots, Sembène trusts the viewer's imagination to prolong his films. This explains his frequent use of freeze-frames, which in a way indicates that the plot goes beyond the actual ending of the motion picture. In such films as "Borom Sarret," "Mandabi," and "Ceddo," he leaves his spectators with a choice between several alternatives as the films end, and the didactic value of such endings is found in the discussion they may trigger after the film screenings. It is interesting to note here that Sembène has stated many times that his films should fulfill the function of a night school for their viewers.

Structurally, the clear linear progression usually found in Sembène's films can also be compared to that of the griot's story (one only notices flashbacks and flash-forwards in "Black Girl" and "Ceddo"). "Mandabi" and "Xala" have the freshness and the atmosphere of tales and parables, while "Emitaï" and "Ceddo" reflect the solemn tone of some of Africa's oral epics. Sembène's use of African languages, songs, palavers, and proverbs confer on his works the same local flavor which can be found in African storytelling. In fact, "Mandabi" was the first West African full-length fiction film ever shot entirely in an African language, a practice which has since been adopted by a number of African filmmakers anxious to underscore the linguistic authenticity of their settings.

Finally, like African tales, Sembène's didactic works are initiatory journeys which cause a new awareness and a basic change in the existential world view of both the protagonist and the viewer. We remember, for instance, in "Mandabi," how Ibrahima Dieng arrives at a new practical wisdom which may, in the future, enable him to cope with his changing milieu. We also recall how "Ceddo" conveys to many spectators new knowledge concerning the Islamic penetration into Senegal. In Ousmane Sembène's disenchanted fables, which denounce and challenge social and political injustice, the social consciousness of his main characters emerges from an acute self-consciousness brought about by the juxtaposition of opposites in the context within which they evolve: the old versus the new, good versus evil, the weak versus the powerful, or poverty versus wealth. Such binary oppositions are found in myths and tales to the extent that one might rightly wonder if the conflicting elements of Sembène's films are not more related to African oral storytelling rather than solely, as many critics have pointed out, to the Marxist components of his ideology.

In spite of using metaphoric tale-like elements with a universal significance, Sembène's cinema is also strongly characterized by its realistic re-creations, and the naturalistic, quasi-documentary facets of its representations. As he writes the plot for a film, Sembène (who is the single author of all of his scripts except that of "Camp de Thiaroye") draws his inspiration from historical facts, as is the case in "Ceddo" and "Emitaï," or from current events. "Niaye" illustrates "a case of incest which actually took place and the young girl had to leave her village."[22] "Black Girl" emerged from the suicide of a black maid which was reported in *Nice-Matin,* a French newspaper shown in the film. As for "Xala," the filmmaker notes that "according to some people the *xala* or spell of impotence does exist."[23]

Anxious to reflect the various facets of Senegalese reality, Sembène's filming techniques and editing change according to what is represented. "Xala," which takes place in an urban environment, has a quicker pace than "Emitaï," which portrays village life styles. And a lot of his motion pictures (e. g. "Niaye," "Ceddo," "Emitaï") are shot outdoors in medium or long shots to illustrate the collective, communal aspect of traditional Senegalese life, in which a person is always in close contact with nature. Sembène's use of languages also adds naturalness and a forceful meaning to his films, as can be observed in "Xala" and "Mandabi." In both films, the use of French by the urban elite and of Wolof by the masses stresses the social gap existing between the two groups, while the use of pidgin French by African soldiers in both "Emitaï" and "Camp de Thiaroye" reflects their alienation as they stand on the edge of two cultures. Likewise, to remain as close as possible to reality, Sembène has elected to use in his films a majority of non-professional actors, preferably coming from the same socio-cultural background as the characters they are made to interpret. Finally, such people as Claire Andrade-Watkins could indeed talk about the care Sembène brings to his historical re-creation. She researched for long months in the United States to find the exact label of the can of corned beef that will be used by soldiers in Sembène's forthcoming motion picture "Samori." I have myself seen in Sembène's Dakar office proof of the elaborate preparations and archival research linked to "Samori": maps, reconstructions of Samori's military camps, and drawings of his soldiers' attire. The late filmmaker and film historian Paulin Soumanou Vieyra, a long-time friend of Sembène, who participated in the making of a number of his films as production manager, used to stress the precision Sembène brings to both his research and his scripts. Vieyra once stated: "Sembène's background as a writer helps him to research and prepare his films with great accuracy. All of his films are interesting because they deal with a great variety of themes proper to Senegalese life."[24]

Not only does Sembène write and direct his films, he adds another personal touch by performing in them as well. In "Black Girl," he plays the role of school master, a character on the edge of tradition and modernity, able to record and to teach the events he has witnessed. He plays the role of the "public letter writer" in "Mandabi," which could be interpreted on a symbolic as well as on a literal level since Sembène is a socially inclined writer, a "public" writer as well as a filmmaker, who records the aspirations and preoccupations of his compatriots. Then, having served in the French colonial army, he is one of "Emitaï's" African soldiers. One could also draw a parallel between Sembène's determination and spirit of resistance and his appearance as a *ceddo* [rebel] in his film "Ceddo." Yet, in his unique way of dismantling the appealing theories of critics, Sembène rejects such assumptions by stressing:

> I kind of like playing in my films, but I do not play roles that are purposely interrelated throughout my works or connected to my personality or my own experience... Pragmatically, my playing in my films encourages the non-professional actors because at the beginning, people in Senegal used to identify actors with the griots, who are people of low caste. In "Ceddo," I was asking people who had been taking care of their hair for years to shave their heads. So I decided to become a *ceddo* myself and to have my head shaved to show solidarity with the actors.[25]

I also asked Sembène whether his appearances in his films could be compared to the way Hitchcock features himself in his own motion pictures, to which Sembène abruptly and vividly stated: "It is not Hitchcock's way; it is Sembène's way."

Many other elements characterize Sembène as a filmmaker and contribute to the uniqueness of his cinema. However, I'd like to conclude my presentation by commenting on his use of comedy and satire, two elements which are omnipresent in the form and content of his films.

Everyone familiar with Sembène's films remembers the truculence of "Xala's" wedding sequence, and recalls the farcical scene in which El Hadji, applying his marabout's prescription against impotence, crawls half naked towards his new wife. Furthermore, a dance scene in which the tiny president of the Chamber of Commerce disappears in the arms and bosom of El Hadji's second wife is hilarious. So is a sequence in which El Hadji's Mercedes-Benz automobile, a product of German engineering genius, has to be pushed by the Senegalese policemen who have come to confiscate it because none of them is able to drive it. Just as striking is the irony used by Sembène in the dinner scene in "Black Girl" where he denounces and mocks the French *petite bourgeoisie* talking about all the advantages that French technical advisers receive from their government's aid program to Senegal (with the benevo- lence of then-President Senghor).

Sembène's use of verbal irony is highly effective in "Camp de Thiaroye" and in "Emitaï," where the soldiers' use of broken French is historically precise, but also effective as a comical device. In "Emitaï," two African soldiers criticize French institutions and question the logic of a system in which Pétain, a seven-star marshal can be replaced by De Gaulle, a lower-ranked brigadier general. The mocking rifleman is Sembène who gives us an unforgettable example of his talents as an actor. Indeed, Sembène's use of satire is unique and expresses the filmmaker's ironic world view and skepticism. For him, life is a series of ambiguities, paradoxes, and incoherences best denounced through biting sarcasm. For the Senegalese director, comedy has a definite function. Commenting on the caricature style of "Xala," he points out:

> Yes, it makes people laugh but it also makes them think. For us, laughter is a social phenomenon: people like to talk and laugh. At the movies, they remember better what has made them laugh than what has made them cry. And there is a lot of discussion taking place as people leave the movie theater.[26]

Ousmane Sembène is one of the pioneers who have sown the seeds of sub-Saharan African cinema. He is its best known representative because of the quality, consistency and personal vision found in his films. Some of the characteristics I have just discussed can indeed be found in the works of other African filmmakers, who may have been influenced by Sembène although they may not readily acknowledge it. Yet, it is his combination of such characteristics which constitutes the uniqueness of Sembène's creativity as filmmaker. His works are landmarks and classics of African cinema to the extent that he has even created "genres" in African filmmaking. In the years to come, no one will discuss African film comedy without mentioning Sembène's film "Xala," and few people will be able to discuss stories of resistance in African cinema without citing "Emitaï" and "Camp de Thiaroye," while the African epic genre on the screen will invariably call to mind "Ceddo."

Of course, Sembène is not the only African director worthy of attention. He is, nevertheless, the one who has accomplished the most, and he has been the most influential participant in the definition of both African film aesthetics and ethics. A socially committed writer, a provocative politically-oriented griot filmmaker, a social activist and critic, Sembène is frequently called the father of sub-Saharan African cinema. His films are primarily intended for African audiences for whom they serve as a tool for progress through self-examination. But for the non-African viewers, Sembène's films are invaluable reflectors of Africa's history, traditions, and changing societies, thus bringing about a new awareness of foreign thought, customs, and aesthetics.

Official History, Popular Memory: Reconfiguration of the African Past in the Films of Ousmane Sembène

by Mbye Cham

HOWARD UNIVERSITY

I would like to begin my presentation by quoting the words of a griot. His name is Diali Mamadou Kouyaté; he performed the *Sundiata* epic, which has been transcribed by Djibril Tamsir Niane. The griot starts his performance with these words:

> I am a griot. . . we are the vessels of speech, we are the repositories which harbor secrets many centuries old. The art of eloquence has no secrets for us; without us, the names of kings would vanish into oblivion, we are the memory of mankind. . . History has no mystery for us. . . for it is we who keep the keys to the twelve doors of Mali. . . I teach kings the history of their ancestors so that the lives of the ancients might serve them as an example. For the world is old, but the future springs from the past.[27]

The last two decades in Africa have yielded a significant crop of films devoted primarily to a critical engagement with the African past as a way of coming to terms with the many crises and challenges confronting contemporary African societies. This current preoccupation with history, and its implications for the present, underlies a number of films which have been produced during these past two decades. Ousmane Sembène, of course, led the way with "Emitaï," "Ceddo," and more recently, "Camp de Thiaroye." This is also a strain that has pretty much defined many of the films of Med Hondo of Mauritania, more specifically, a film he produced in 1978 entitled "West Indies," which is an adaptation of a play with the same title by a Martinican playwright, Daniel Boukman, and Hondo's latest film, entitled "Sarraounia," which came out in 1986. Also in this category is a recent film produced by a young filmmaker from Guinea-Bissau, whose name is Flora Gomes. The title of the film is "Mortu Nega," and it is a reconstruction of the recent history of Guinea-Bissau during and after the armed liberation struggle against Portuguese colonialism. There is also a young Malagasy filmmaker, Raymond Rajaonarivelo, who in 1988 came out with another film that reconstructs an event that took place in the context of the Second World War in the Malagasy Republic, and the title of that film is "Tabataba." We also have two recent films from Ghana. One is by a young Ghanaian filmmaker who is currently residing in London. His name is John Akomfrah; his 1988 film entitled "Testament" looks at the Nkrumah era in Ghana. The other one, "Heritage Africa," also a 1988 film, is by Kwaw Ansah.

So dominant is this current in contemporary African filmmaking that one is reminded of a statement made by Jorge Fraga, a Cuban filmmaker and member of the Cuban Film Institute: "Cuban filmmakers are always viewing things from a historical perspective because, 'we can't help it.'"[28] Judging from the recently finished films, as well as a number of projects that are currently in production, it seems that African filmmakers too cannot help but look at things from a historical perspective. The necessity of looking at the present in the past is made urgent by the fact that the histories of former colonies have been characterized by arbitrary fictions, fictions such as the White Man's Burden, Manifest Destiny, Hegel's Africa beyond the pale of history, repeated by Hugh Trevor-Roper's notion of history in Africa as only the history of Europeans in Africa, and so on and so forth. And because of these fictions, African filmmakers and other artists have taken on the task of purging their histories of these imposed remembrances. In turning to the pre-colonial and colonial past, many contemporary African filmmakers repeat, with a significant difference of course, the gestures of an earlier generation of African artists, who in their various ways responded to prevailing Western fictions and orthodoxies about Africa and Africans by effecting a return to the sources in the form of counter-accounts and reconstructions of Africa before the arrival of Europeans.

Early in this century—in the twenties, thirties, and forties—some African poets and novelists developed Négritude and other cognate rallying cries and ideologies as a framework for delving into the African past in order to intervene in and alter dominant Eurocentric versions of Africa and Africans by introducing different African versions of Africa and Africans. I don't wish to explore here how authentic these Négritude versions of Africa and Africans were, but the point I am interested in is the act of looking back as a means of coming to terms with current prevailing beliefs and orientations and challenges in Africa. While the contemporary African filmmaker repeats the historical moves of his Négritude predecessor, he does so with a different set of ideologies and orientations, a different conception of history and tradition, and under a different set of social, political, and cultural circumstances. Given these differences, what emerges in recent African film is a radical revision and representation of the African past in ways which not only purge it of imposed European and other foreign remembrances, but which also foreground the relevance of the new reconstructed histories to the present challenges of post-colonial African societies.

It is not an exaggeration to claim that the principal force behind this orientation in African film is Ousmane Sembène, whose films, especially "Emitaï," "Ceddo," and more recently, "Camp de Thiaroye," constitute some of the most compelling and indeed radical filmic revisions and reinterpretations of history in Africa. Particularly noteworthy in these new film versions of history are:

a) The recovery and deployment of popular memory to recompose past events.
b) The radical reconstruction of Euro-Christian as well as Arab-Islamic histories and how these are implicated in African history.
c) The conflation of Euro-Christianity and Arab-Islam as two sides of the same colonial coin.
d) The national as well as the pan-African nature and dimension of these histories.
e) The recovery and reconstitution of African women's histories—from a male point of view, of course.

I had wanted to consider these and related issues as well as their modes of representation in "Ceddo," "Emitaï," and "Camp de Thiaroye," but because of the limitation of time, I am going to focus only on "Ceddo." I would like to echo here the words of Diali Mamadou Kouyaté, which I have quoted at the beginning, with the words of another noted African elder and intellectual from Mali, whose name is Amadou Hampathé Bâ. Amadou Hampathé Bâ has stated the following:

> The fact that it has no system of writing does not in itself deprive Africa of a past or of a body of knowledge. . . Of course, this body of inherited knowledge that is transmitted from the mouth of one generation to the ear of the next may either grow or wither away. . . The African body of knowledge is vast and varied, and it touches on all aspects of life. The "knowledge expert" is never a "specialist" but a generalist. . . The African body of knowledge is thus a *comprehensive* and living knowledge, and that is why the old men who are its last trustees can be compared to vast libraries where multifarious bookshelves are linked to each other by invisible connections which are the essence of the "science of the invisible."[29]

It was in reference to the urgency of recovering and deploying the knowledge and wisdom of this last generation of great depositories, this living memory of Africa, that Hampathé Bâ made his now canonical statement that in Africa an old person who dies is a library that burns. The filmic reconstruction of history, in the work of Ousmane Sembène, rests solidly on this heritage of oral tradition and memory. From this base, with the true griot as a model, Sembène enters into a battle for history and around history. Official versions of the past, Western as well as Arabic, are contested, revised, and/or rejected, and new, more authentic histories are put in their place.

Sembène's films may partly be seen as undertaking what Teshome Gabriel has labeled "a rescue mission," to the extent to which their recourse to popular memory aims to recover, privilege and articulate the historical significance and the contemporary, as well as future, implications of what official histories insist on erasing. My conception of the notions of popular memory and official history owes a great deal to Teshome Gabriel's elaboration of these concepts:

> Official history tends to arrest the future by means of the past. Historians privilege the written word of the text—it serves as their rule of law. It claims a "center" which continuously marginalizes others. In this way its ideology inhibits people from constructing their own history or histories.
>
> Popular memory, on the other hand, considers the past as a political issue. It orders the past not only as a reference point but also as a theme of struggle. For popular memory, there are no longer any "centers" or "margins," since the very designations imply that something has been conveniently left out.[30]

Then, echoing a widely articulated Third World view, Teshome Gabriel has argued that

> Popular memory, then, is neither a retreat to some great tradition nor a flight to some imagined "ivory tower," neither a self-indulgent escapism, nor a desire for the actual "experience" or "content" of the past for its own sake. Rather, it is a "look back to the future," necessarily dissident and partisan, wedded to constant change.[31]

"Ceddo," "Emitaï," and "Camp de Thiaroye," each in its own way, embody the spirit of popular memory. "Ceddo" is a film that re-creates the structures of power and power relations in the nineteenth-century Wolof state of Joloff, on the eve of its demise at the hands of Islam, in competition at times with Christianity and its ally, French commercial and secular power. The privileged point of view in this film is clearly the *ceddo*'s, and it inscribes itself in popular memory. Foregrounding this hitherto repressed point of view results in the explosion by Sembène of a solidly entrenched official version of history of Islam in Senegal. According to this version, Islam is Senegalese. In other versions that concede its non-Senegalese origins, it is posited that Islam's mode of entry into Senegal was all peaceful. Another aspect of this official version states that Islam was voluntarily espoused by the Senegalese, who were won over by exponents of redemption and salvation. In "Ceddo," therefore, the term "official" takes on a new meaning, beyond its usual designation of that which is French or French-derived, which is the dominant conception of what is official in Senegal and also in many other African countries. It is no longer a monopoly of the French.

In the same breath, Sembène also enlarges the field of foreign colonial actors in Senegal beyond the French, as is the case in "Emitaï" and "Camp de Thiaroye," to expose the other equally significant and deadly force which has succeeded in passing itself off as Senegalese, namely Islam. Unlike a good number of his fellow Senegalese, who tend to subscribe to Islam's claim to indigenous antiquity in Senegal, Sembène presents Islam in "Ceddo" as one of the forces—the other being Euro-Christianity, of course—responsible for what Wole Soyinka refers to as "Africa's enforced cultural and political exocentricity."[32] Customs, beliefs, values, and practices, hitherto presented and taken as Senegalese or African, are examined and shown to be of Arab-Islamic origin by Sembène in "Ceddo." Moreover, the process by which these Arab-Islamic customs, beliefs, values, and practices came to take root in Senegal is presented as insidious and violent, not unlike the ways in which Euro-Christian slavery, colonialism, and imperialism bulldozed their way into Senegal. Thus, Sembène counteracts the official Senegalese-Islamic version of the West as the sole source of Africa's cultural contamination and degradation with a new version which splits Islam's roots away from Senegalese soil, casts Islam as heavily infused with Arab culture, and conflates it with Euro-Christianity. "Ceddo" is therefore the most irreverent rewriting of Islam in Senegal by a Senegalese artist. It reconstructs its history in Senegal in ways that radically destabilize and undo the dominant Islamic myth espoused by the Muslim elite and their followers, who happen to be the majority of the Senegalese.

In "Ceddo," the image of Islam that is portrayed is not a beautiful one at all. The Muslims are presented as scheming, violent fanatics with little regard for the principles of self-determination and religious and cultural freedom. Their belief in the supremacy of Islam is translated into a series of highly studied moves, which systematically eliminate the rival Christian mission, the traditional secular power structure, and a significant number of the *ceddo* and their belief systems. This project culminates in the establishment of a regime of rule based on principles of Islam, with the imam as the head. The designs of the imam on the society are progressively made clear in the course of the narrative in "Ceddo." His initial litany of verbal attacks on the persistence of pagan practices among the *ceddo* is indirectly pointed at the Wolof secular authority, the King, who is now a convert, yet who tolerates the presence of such infidels, as he calls them, in his society. These attacks become more pointed as the militancy of the Muslims intensifies and as the imam's vow to undertake a jihad against all non-Muslims in the society looms closer to execution. To the King's question as to why the imam never addresses him by the title "King," the imam replies that for him there is only one king, and that king is Allah. To the *ceddo*'s complaint about the growing harassment from the Muslims, and to their question as to whether religion is worth a man's life, the imam, usurping the prerogative and power of the King, shouts blasphemy and renews his threats against them. This attitude defines the relationship of the imam to the society around him, and it sets the stage for embarking on a *jihad* to bring about the rule of Allah. The Muslims burn down the Christian mission and kill the white missionary and the trader, from whom they had obtained their weapons. Next, the news is announced that the King has died from a snake bite; as a consequence the *ceddo* are subdued and forcibly converted to Islam. Into the power vacuum created by the death of the Wolof king steps the imam. Thus, Sembène reconstructs the origin of, and the reasons for, the absence of traditional secular power figures and structures, and the hegemonic status and power of Muslim marabouts and brotherhoods in Senegal today.

In "Ceddo," the imam's ascension to power marks the beginning of what Sembène conveys in the film as one of the most radical and intolerant projects of cultural transformation in Senegalese history. The imam institutes as law most of the spiritual and social conduct hitherto adhered to by only a tiny minority. Among the practices of the *ceddo* that are prohibited under the new Muslim theocracy are the consumption of alcohol, the reproduction of human forms in art, and former modes of worship. The Islamic regime of five daily prayers, the *shahada*, and koranic education become mandatory. The griot of the erstwhile royal court, together with his cronies, is unceremoniously dismissed and replaced by the koran-toting disciples of the imam. The high point of this process of social and cultural change comes in the mass conversion sequence of the film, where the *ceddo* are subdued and submitted to a ritual of purification as a prerequisite for assuming new Muslim identities. They have their heads shaved clean and their *ceddo* names are replaced by new Arab or Arab-derived names, such as Hadidiatou, Fatoumata, Mamadou, Souleymane, Babacar, and Ousmane. Historical reconstruction in "Ceddo," then, privileges a non-Muslim perspective, one that is repressed in official accounts of Islam in Senegal. It explores a deeply ingrained myth in Senegalese society. Sembène's own attitude towards this myth is most graphically defined in the final sequence when Dior Yacine, the princess, heir to the throne, kills the imam with a shotgun, in full view of his disciples and the new converts. Thus Sembène rewrites and represents, in a radically different view, a much neglected aspect of the historical role of women in African history. In "Ceddo," Princess Dior is posited as a figure of resistance and liberation. The amount of screen time that she occupies in the film is rather limited, and we only hear her voice in relatively few sequences. However, in spite of these physical absences, Princess Dior is the overwhelming presence in the film. The narrative turns and moves around her captivity. And it is she who emerges from her position of royalty—captured royalty nevertheless—to rekindle and put in action the *ceddo* spirit of resistance and refusal of domination. This is captured symbolically in the final sequence of the film which ends—and I put "ends" in quotes here, because the film never actually ends—in a half-shot freeze-frame, with her occupying the larger portion of the screen.

Historical reconstruction, then, in "Ceddo," aims to explore deeply ingrained myths in Senegalese society. "Ceddo" may be unique in Senegalese artistic percep-tions of Islam and the history of Islam, in terms of its tone, its tenor, and its uncompromising view of the religion. But it is indicative of a growing current of thought, both in African literature and in African film. One is reminded of the equally caustic savaging of Islam in Yambo Ouologuem's *Le devoir de violence*, Ayi Kwei Armah's *Two Thousand Seasons*, and elsewhere in Chancellor Williams's *The Destruction of Black Civilization*.

Film Production in Francophone Africa 1961 to 1977: Ousmane Sembène—An Exception[33]

by Claire Andrade-Watkins

EMERSON COLLEGE

Introduction

The advent of independence throughout francophone Africa in 1960 ushered in an era of transition for France and her former colonies. France provided development assistance and technical expertise to former francophone African colonies through the Ministry of Cooperation, created expressly for the newly independent countries.[34] In cinema, financial and technical assistance was provided on two levels: The *Consortium Audiovisuel International* (CAI), the private sector arm of the Ministry of Cooperation established in 1961, produced newsreels, educational documentaries, and other special projects for the former colonies; the *Bureau du Cinéma* (Film Bureau), on the other hand, provided financial and technical assistance to African filmmakers.

The Film Bureau, from its creation in 1963 through the 1979 restructuring of the Ministry of Cooperation, provided the technical and financial assistance which made francophone Africa the most prolific center of black African cinema. Not a single feature film was made by an African prior to independence, yet by 1975 over 185 shorts and features had been produced with the technical and financial assistance of the Film Bureau. As a result, eighty percent of all black African films were being made by francophone Africans.[35] This perspective is broadened by Ousmane Sembène, who is widely acclaimed as the father of African cinema, and as the leading proponent of *cinéma engagé*—a militant, Marxist challenge to the African bourgeoisie, to French neo-colonialism, and to the insidious role of Islam and Christianity in African society. The juxtaposition of Sembène and his work to the larger context of French post-colonial ministerial programs for cinema in sub-Saharan francophone Africa illuminates key contradictions and ironies for African cinema during the era under consideration.

In order to gain a better understanding of this pivotal period of African cinema in general and francophone Africa in particular, we shall now turn to the operations of France's Ministry of Cooperation between 1961 and 1977.

Historical Overview of Francophone Africa 1961 to 1977

Although *de jure* independence was granted to francophone Africa, *de facto* political, economic, and cultural ties to the former French colonies remained a priority for the French government. Unlike the English, who preferred to maintain a distance between themselves and their African subjects, the French pulled their subjects into the francophone culture. France's colonial policy of direct rule and assimilation perpetuated the idea that France and the colonies were a family, bound by the French language and culture. Through a process of education and immersion in the French culture, francophone Africans, particularly African elites and their children, were indoctrinated to view France as the mother country and the Gauls as their ancestors. For France, the emphasis on cultural assimilation was the dominant colonial policy, and it was in that context that economic and political relationships with the colonies were determined. It was a bond the French were unwilling to relinquish at the end of the colonial era.

The importance attached by France to maintaining the post-colonial cultural, economic, and political ties is evidenced by the creation of the Ministry of Cooperation in 1961 by the De Gaulle government. Through the Ministry critical financial and technical resources were provided to the former colonies, and this preserved France's dominance in the region—culturally, linguistically, and economically. The Ministry was primarily responsible for economic, cultural, and technical assistance to the former colonies in areas requiring technical specialization and expertise such as agronomy, diplomacy, and filmmaking.[36]

Sub-Saharan francophone Africa—with Senegal at the epicenter of the activity—dominated African cinema ideologically, quantitatively, and qualitatively. Three factors account for this dominance. First, there was the creation of the CAI and the Film Bureau. Second, francophone Africa was home to major pioneers of African cinema—including the Senegalese filmmaker/historian Paulin Vieyra and Ousmane Sembène, creator of the first feature made by an African, "La noire de. . ." Lastly, it was francophone Africa which provided much of the leadership for FEPACI (*Fédération Panafricaine des Cinéastes*), the thirty-three country member organization of African filmmakers which was established in 1969.

Administration of the Film Bureau

Created in 1963 within the Ministry itself, the Film Bureau in turn worked with the CAI on the educational documentary series for francophone Africa. The major mission of the Bureau, however, as the largest producer of African cinema during this period, was to provide technical and financial resources to individual African filmmakers to create works of "cultural" expression.

The creation of the Bureau was actually preceded by a general cinema service within the Ministry. Lucien Patry, the creator of the *Section Technique* within what became the Film Bureau, was recruited in early 1962 to organize a cinema service that would address in some logical fashion the technical needs of the films or projects by filmmakers—African as well as French—sociologists, ethnologists, geographers, or *coopérants* of the Ministry, as they made films in the newly independent African states. Patry rapidly went about setting up a small 16mm production center, with editing tables and sound transfer equipment, the basic minimum needed to provide technical support to the work coming in. Several months later, in 1963, Patry's small technical section was set up as a separate administrative entity, the Film Bureau.[37]

Although the organization became the largest producer of African cinema, its actual full-time staff always remained small, increasing from five or six people at the beginning to a maximum of twelve. The key personnel involved with African cinema were the director, Debrix; Lucien Gohy, who worked at the Bureau from 1966 to 1976, first with the educational documentaries done by the CAI and the Bureau, then as Debrix's assistant; and Patry, who was in charge of the *Section Technique*. In addition to supervising the technical end of the Bureau's operations, Patry was also responsible for hiring the freelance technicians. Not all staff worked directly with African cinema; others worked on projects or tasks associated with the 16mm educational and documentary projects of the CAI which were edited at the Film Bureau.[38]

The crux of the issue arose when the technical and financial support provided by the Bureau in exchange for France's cultural products became a liability for France's politics of cultural development. Perhaps not during the early years of the Bureau's operations but by the early 1970s, the Bureau was becoming a costly political liability. It is clear that in giving assistance to cultural expression, the Bureau did not foresee the inevitable conflicts which were going to arise from its policies. The Bureau came under increasing attack from two sides: on one side were the African filmmakers, who criticized the Bureau's non-commercial distribution of their work and also pushed for better services and greater financial and technical assistance; on the other side, the Ministry of Cooperation and some of the African governments attacked the Bureau for providing support to films which they considered critical of or detrimental to governmental authority.[39]

It is a well-known fact that the Film Bureau provided financial and technical assistance to African filmmakers in exchange for the non-commercial rights to their films.[40] What is not so apparent are the criteria used and formulas applied in determining the financial and technical support. In the actual operations of the Bureau there were concrete checks and balances within the administrative process as well as established procedures for providing technical and financial assistance which were logical and had a bottom line accountability.

The Bureau used two major policy precautions to minimize the economic and particularly the political risk factors involved in providing technical and financial assistance. First, funds for individual projects were rarely released directly to the African filmmakers; rather the allocated amount remained within the Bureau and was applied directly to the costs of the technical services, labs, editors, and sound mixing of a project which was billed to the Bureau.[41] The second major policy precaution at the Bureau was a strong preference for completed films or works in progress.

Areas of financial and technical assistance have been separated so that different perspectives could be highlighted. In actuality, however, the purchase of the non-commercial rights, the project selection, and the assistance package were integrally related. A major administrative objective (which differs from the political consider-ations noted earlier) was to look at the work or project in order to determine whether technically there was a reasonable possibility that it could be completed. If the assessment made was that the assistance needed was reasonable and within the means of the Bureau, a package was put together and a contract was drawn up between the Film Bureau and the producer, who could be either the filmmaker or a third party acting on behalf of the filmmaker. The assistance package included a combination of money, materials, and services, with the Bureau emphasizing materials and services over money.

Ousmane Sembène: The Exception and the Irony

Pressure on the French government and the Ministry of Cooperation by the African filmmakers for the reasons cited above accelerated the decline of the Film Bureau. The creation in 1969 of FEPACI and aggressive lobbying efforts for more assistance to African filmmakers and access to the lucrative commercial market for their films, as well as internal ministerial criticism, forced the French to re-evaluate their policies concerning cinema in particular as well as the overall Cooperative program of the Ministry.

Filmmakers with Marxist or critical perspectives, like Ousmane Sembène, did not gain access to the financial and technical resources provided by the CAI or the Film Bureau—both creations of the Ministry of Cooperation.

Sembène and his work posed a major dilemma for Debrix and the Bureau. Debrix had actually turned away Sembène when he originally approached the Bureau for guidance in studying film. Then later, he also turned down Sembène's scenario for "La noire de. . .," the first feature to be done by an African. Ironically, therefore, the first helping hand to one of the greatest African filmmakers came not from the Bureau but from André Zwobada, a highly respected French film professional with very powerful ministerial connections.[42]

Zwobada, someone Debrix credits with being a figure instrumental in the birth of African cinema, does not return those generous accolades to Debrix or the Bureau:

> *...Alors qu'est ce qu'il a dit...il a dit une simple phrase: "Ainsi fut-il porté assistance non seulement aux films de Sembène mais encore à l'un de ses plus chauds supporters, (c'est moi le supporter) un homme dont on ignore trop qu'il a été avec Jean Rouch (ça ce n'est pas vrai, Rouch n'a rien à voir là-dedans), à la naissance du jeune cinéma négro-africain." Je n'ai assisté à aucune naissance, je n'ai rien vu.*[43]

[...Well, what did he say... He just said a sentence: "In this way help was given not only to Sembène's films but also to one of his strongest supporters (that means me), a man who should be much better known for having been present, together with Jean Rouch (that is not true; Rouch had nothing to do with this), at the birth of black African cinema." I was not present at any birth. I did not see anything.]

Zwobada, a seasoned French film professional, who also served as the chief editor of the *Actualités Françaises*, is highly contemptuous of Debrix and the whole concept of African cinema. Referring again to the statements by Debrix in the same article, Zwobada goes on to comment that Debrix had to cite him as one of the notable people in the birth of African cinema or the reality of the Bureau would be exposed as a travesty. This cryptic comment refers to the fact that Zwobada, in his capacity as the head of the *Actualités Françaises*, the newsreel service of the government, made it possible for Sembène to film and edit his first films, and more importantly his first feature, "La noire de...," which was the first feature done by an African.[44] He also arranged for post-production editing to occur at the *Actualités Françaises* facilities at Geneville.

This of course is a *cause célèbre*: it is one of the ironies of the Film Bureau that the work of one of the greatest African filmmakers was not "brought to birth" by the Bureau, although the Bureau ultimately purchased the rights for non-commercial distribution of the film throughout those countries that were members of the French community. As one of Africa's leading exponents of *cinéma engagé*, Sembène created a tremendous stir in the governments of France and Africa through his films, which were profound Marxist critiques of African bourgeois corruption and France's neo-colonialism.

Zwobada's assistance to Sembène stemmed from his high personal regard for Sembène and his talent. Zwobada was intrigued and interested enough by Sembène and his work to set a precedent, which Zwobada could do because he had the means at his disposal.[45] Moreover, he was able to convince the Ministry of Cooperation that his support was in line with the policy for "African cultural development," and that the French could take credit for this.

The contact between Sembène and Zwobada was made by Paulin Vieyra, the director of the *Actualités Sénégalaises*, the government newsreel service. Through his connections with the Ministry of Cooperation and the CAI, Vieyra was able to introduce his friend Sembène to Zwobada, and the rest was history or, as Zwobada says, a *coup de foudre*. Although Sembène's future productions were to be realized with different means through his private company, Zwobada's intervention in the early films was pivotal in launching Sembène's work.[46]

Having served as a director himself, as well as an assistant to Jean Renoir, Zwobada looks askance at the Bureau, blaming it and Debrix for giving the African filmmakers false expectations. Zwobada points out many of the political, philosophical and ideological contradictions within the Bureau:

> *Ce que je veux dire c'est que ce brave Debrix, qui est mort, paix à son âme, pensait que le cinéma africain pourrait naître en donnant de l'argent, en arrosant d'un peu d'argent partout. C'est prendre le système dans le mauvais sens. Le vrai sens c'est de produire un film et qu'il passe dans les salles. Mais donner à tous ces gens des espoirs qui sont faux! Ce n'est pas parce que vous donnez de l'argent à quelqu'un (au contraire, je crois qu'il ne faut pas lui donner de l'argent, il faut qu'il se débrouille tout seul, qu'il se batte comme Sembène s'est battu), mais. . .Et il y avait aussi une arrière pensée colonialiste dans tout ça. C'est à dire la France, la francophonie, etc. Et quand, avec Sembène, on a fait "La noire de. . . ," ils étaient furieux. Ils pensaient que c'était contre la France. J'ai dit, "Non, ce n'est pas contre la France, c'est l'expression de gens qui ont subi la France." Maintenant, ils pensent qu'ils sont libres. Debrix m'a dit "Mais comment avez-vous pu donner de l'argent pour ça, c'est contre la France. . ." Je lui ai dit qu'à partir du moment où l'on mélange cette question de propagande politique de la France, il n'y aura jamais de cinéma africain, ce n'est pas possible. Alors tout ça c'est bien gentil, mais. . . J'avais de l'argent aux Actualités Françaises.*[47]

[What I mean is that the good Debrix—who has died, may his soul rest in peace—thought that African cinema could get a start if he gave some money, if he watered the soil everywhere with a little money. That is doing things the wrong way round. The right way is to produce a film and then see that it gets into the theaters. But it is not right to awaken false hopes in all these people! You don't get any results by giving someone money (on the contrary, I believe you should not give money. The person should make it on his own, should have to fight for what he wants, as Sembène had to do) but. . . Moreover, in all this there was a hidden colonialist agenda: of France, of francophonie, and so on. When we made "Black Girl" with Sembène, they were furious. They thought the film was directed against France. I told them, "No, it's not directed against France, it expresses the feelings of people who had France imposed on them." Now they consider themselves free. Debrix said to me, "But how could you give money for such a project directed against France. . ." I replied that once this question of French political propaganda was brought in, there would never be an African cinema at all. This was all very well, but. . . I had funds available at the *Actualités Françaises*.]

Sembène continued on to become one of the first African filmmakers to establish his own production company, Domirev, through which he either produced or co-produced his other films, again preserving his autonomy. With "Mandabi" in 1968, Sembène was the first African to receive funds from the *Centre National de la Cinématographie*, which required that he work with a French co-producer, *Comptoir Français du Film*. He insisted on and established a precedent of shooting the film in both French and Wolof. "Emitaï" in 1971 was a Domirev production; "Xala" in 1974 a co-production with the *Société Nationale du Cinéma* created by Senegal. It was one of four films produced between 1974 and 1976 in one of the first but short-lived efforts of African governmental support to African filmmakers. "Ceddo" was also a distinctly unique production package, realized as a co-production between Domirev, the state, and the bank.

All of Sembène's films, even in this somewhat eclectic period of financial and technical assistance, maintained a degree of integrity, boldness and autonomy which is as distinctive as the content of the films he produced.

Conclusion

The power of the Ministry of Cooperation was sharply curtailed and dramatically restructured following the political upheavals in the late 1970s. The rise of the Socialist government of François Mitterand in 1981 resulted in a shift of emphasis of the French state from technical and financial assistance to individual countries, to a broader focus which would work through the regional grouping of francophone African states as represented by OCAM (*Organisation Commune Africaine et Mauricienne*). The objective was to begin to provide assistance which would lead to regional self-sufficiency. The Film Bureau came under closer scrutiny by the French government and was increasingly perceived as a political liability, particularly because it provided technical and financial assistance to individual filmmakers, which at times created political problems between France and disgruntled African governments angered by the content of some of the films.

The subsequent restructuring under Mitterand effectively dismantled the power and autonomy of the Ministry of Cooperation. Rather than working through the Film Bureau, the Mitterand government shifted assistance to the CIDC (*Comité Interafricain de Distribution Cinématographique*), CIPROFILM (*Consortium Interafricain de Production de Film*) and INAFEC (*Institut Africain d'Etudes Cinématographiques*) which were established in francophone Africa to encourage regional infrastructures in distribution, production and technical film training.[48]

As black African cinema moves into its third decade, the obstacles to financial and technical self-sufficiency in production, distribution and exhibition have largely remained unresolved. Efforts to establish national film structures, or regional centers for distribution, exhibition and production have not resulted in viable, stable, and profitable ventures capable of supporting an independent African cinema. Filmmakers must still piece together the financial and technical package from largely foreign sources in order to produce their films, which in many instances still remain inaccessible to African audiences, due to the continued monopoly on commercial theaters held by European companies throughout francophone Africa. This does not infer that there is no hope for an autonomous African cinema, yet it reaffirms the piecemeal, displaced, and precarious process. Ancillary—not incidental—concerns about the paucity of scholarship and criticism of African cinema, minimal support from African governments for the African film industry and its filmmakers, and lack of access to African film audiences remain endemic issues for African cinema today.[49]

Yet an African cinema is emerging from within, drawing on oral traditions, on indigenous languages, and on a growing body of African literature. This is happening in spite of or perhaps because of the obstacles in production, distribution and exhibition. A significant part of the history of African cinema lies within the search for resources and how African filmmakers surmounted the obstacles and detours along the way.

The salient details of those pioneering precedents established by Ousmane Sembène in securing the financial and technical resources to produce his films underscore the concomitant ironies and dilemmas his work presented to the cinematic initiatives launched by France through the Ministry of Cooperation in sub-Saharan Africa. Sembène's pioneering vision, revolutionary both in process and product, has left an indelible imprint on the 1961 to 1977 era and on the history of African cinema.

Ousmane Sembène Responds to Questions from the Audience

Question: Did you write the dialogue in "Emitaï" directly in Diola or did the peasants choose those words with precision themselves? In other words does the dialogue in "Emitaï" represent a translation or is it the first version in the original language?

Sembène: *"Emitaï" était écrit en diola. J'ai préparé les textes et les paysans ont joué. Il faut savoir dans le métier de réalisateur le rapport qu'il y a entre le réalisateur, les gens qui jouent et qui ne sont pas des professionnels, et la langue. Cela fait donc un triangle. Donc j'ai travaillé avec des paysans diola authentiques qui n'avaient jamais vu de cinéma, qui n'avaient jamais été au cinéma. Je peux employer un mot, mais il ne me satisfait pas. J'ai mis deux ans pour les "apprivoiser." Et à ma connaissance, c'est la première fois que les Diola, après le film, ont eux-mêmes entendu leur langue.*

Je n'arrive pas à comprendre la raison de cette question, mais je peux dire que pour mon travail il n'y a aucun conflit d'une langue à l'autre. Pour ceux qui connaissent le Sénégal, et en particulier la Casamance, dès notre enfance nous parlons tous trois ou quatre langues, tant les rapports entre les cultures diola, sossé, wolof et créole sont étroits. Ce qui fait donc que pour nous, nous avons une culture tout à fait enclavée. Mais, malheureusement, actuellement en 1990, petit à petit le diola s'effrite. Il risque de disparaître. D'autres cultures plus envahissantes sont en train de le dominer.

Sur le plan de la conquête coloniale, jusqu'en 1942, les Diola n'étaient pas soumis à la colonisation française. Et ils sont ceux qui ont le plus résisté pendant la lutte de libération de la Guinée Bissau. Et les femmes diola ont opposé plus de résistance sur place aux colonisateurs que les hommes. Donc voilà tout mon rapport avec la langue, mais je suis issu de ce milieu. Ce serait maladroit de montrer ces paysans diola parlant un français académique. En tout cas, personnellement, je n'ai pas de problème de langue avec mon peuple. Et je suis même très gêné quand je parle français aux gens de mon peuple, ce qui m'oblige à apprendre encore des langues. Et voilà, j'ai répondu à la question.

["Emitaï" was written in Diola. I prepared the texts and the peasants did the acting. In the trade of filmmakers you have to know the relationship between the filmmaker, those who play a part but are not professional actors, and the language. That makes a triangle. So I worked with genuine Diola farmers who were never inside a movie theater, who never saw a film before. It took me two years to win them over.

Kango Láre-Lantone (translator), Ousmane Sembène, Samba Gadjigo

Ngugi wa Thiong'o, Toni Cade Bambara, John Wideman, Earl Lovelace, Thomas Cassirer

Photo credits: Gigi Kaeser

Kango Láre-Lantone, Ousmane Sembène, Samba Gadjigo, Ngugi wa Thiong'o

Toni Cade Bambara, Ralph Faulkingham, John Wideman, Earl Lovelace

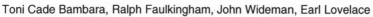

Photo credits: Gigi Kaeser

As far as I know this was the first time, once the film was made, that the Diola could hear themselves speaking their language.

I don't understand the reason behind this question, but I can say that in my work there is no conflict from one language to the other. Those who know Senegal and, in particular, the Casamance region are aware that from early childhood we all speak three or four languages. This shows how closely the Creole, Sossé, Diola and Wolof cultures are intertwined. It means that we have a culture which is completely hemmed in by other cultures. It is unfortunate that today, in 1990, Diola is slowly disintegrating. It's at risk of disappearing and other, more dominant cultures are taking over.

Until 1942, the Diola people did not accept French colonial rule, and they were the people who resisted most strongly during the liberation struggle of Guinea Bissau. The Diola women gave stronger support to this resistance against the colonizers than the men. And that is all there is to my connection with the language, but it is the environment I come from. It would have been clearly inappropriate to have those Diola peasants speaking "proper" French. Anyway, I personally have no language problem with my people, and I am very ill at ease when I do speak French to them. This forces me to learn still more languages. And that is my answer to this question.]

Question: This question concerns the manner in which you turn around the history of Islam in Senegal and give the opposite of the official version. It was not always a very positive history and that is what you show. Does this mean we should view "Ceddo" as a confrontation or even a deconstruction of the history of Sundiata? I am interested in hearing your opinion on this overturning of the written record of the epic of Sundiata.

Sembène: *Mais je pense que peut-être je n'ai pas bien saisi la question. Je pense qu'il y a une grande différence entre Soundjata et la religion musulmane. Ainsi en ce qui concerne la religion musulmane, en 1990, elle fait partie intégrante de la civilisation sénégalaise. Si nous reconnaissons l'Islam, qui est étranger à l'Afrique, et pourquoi ne pas reconnaître la civilisation chrétienne qui est étrangère aussi mais que nous assimilons très bien. Je vais vous apporter peut-être une information: En 1993, à venir, il va y avoir pour la première fois le conseil des églises noires, et qui vont adopter les traditions, les danses et tout pour la cérémonie religieuse. Donc voilà une société consciente d'une chose qui existe, qu'elle assume et qu'elle absorbe.*

Comme le symbolise "Ceddo," nous allons vers le syncrétisme. Est-ce que c'est une faiblesse ou une force de la culture africaine? Je dirais que c'est la force de la culture africaine. Rien ne nous est étranger, nous devons le prendre et le transformer, pour qu'il soit nôtre.

Quant à Soundjata, c'est un grand moment de l'histoire africaine. Il faut l'analyser, le comprendre, et nous en servir maintenant et pour les générations à venir. Voilà donc les réponses que j'avais à cette question.

[I think perhaps I have not fully understood the question. I believe there is a great difference between Sundiata and the Muslim religion. As far as Islam is concerned, it is an integral part of Senegalese civilization in 1990. If we accept Islam, which is foreign to Africa, then why not accept Christian civilization which also is foreign to Africa and which we assimilate very well. Perhaps I am giving you some information that is new to you: In 1993, for the first time, a council of black churches will be held that will adopt African traditions, dances and so on for religious worship. So there you have a society that is aware of what exists, that takes it as its own and absorbs it.

As symbolized by "Ceddo," we are moving towards syncretism. Is this a weakness of African culture or a sign of its strength? I would say that it shows its strength. Nothing is foreign to us; we have to seize and transform it to make it ours.

As far as the story of Sundiata is concerned, it marks a great moment of African history. It has to be analyzed, understood, and applied to the present and for coming generations.]

Question: The chief in "Ceddo," who follows Islam and observes its practices, is someone you do not describe as a particularly heroic character. I suppose you mean to have him serve as an example of many other chiefs or kings and that any one of these kings, such as Sundiata, may belong to this group of rulers.

Sembène: *Non! Il ne faut pas confondre les époques. Si vous aviez le temps de faire la recherche nécessaire, vous n'auriez pas confondu l'histoire de "Ceddo" avec celle de Soundjata. Et je vous demanderais une fois chez vous d'aller faire des recherches.*

      [No! We should not get the time periods mixed up. If you had taken the time to do the necessary research, you would not have confused the history of "Ceddo" with that of Sundiata. And I would ask you to do that research once you get home.]

Question: What was the manner by which Islam was introduced into the Sudan? Did it differ from one period to another?

Sembène: *Mais quel Soudan? Le Soudan veut dire le pays des noirs. Quelle partie de l'Afrique? De l'Est, de l'Ouest ou du Nord? Dans la partie ouest de l'Afrique nous situons cela vers le dixième siècle. Et pour arriver au Sénégal il fallait compter à peu près un siècle. Comment l'Islam s'est introduit, c'est très difficile à dire. Il s'est infiltré lentement, lentement. Parce que malheureusement ceux de mon peuple—je m'excuse d'utiliser le mot "noir," à défaut d'autre chose—mes ancêtres, nourris de leur propre culture, très imbéciles parce que trop généreux, les ont accueillis, nourris, leur ont donné même des épouses, et les ont fait accrocher aux rois, ceux qui commandent, qui incarnent l'autorité. Mais malheureusement, comme des termites, ils ont travaillé de l'intérieur.*

Vous connaissez l'expansion de toutes les religions, spécialement de l'Islam.

Les Arabes vous donnent l'Hégire comme référence historique. L'Hégire, c'est l'année où Mahomet a quitté la Mecque pour la Médina. La Mecque c'est toute une ville, Médina c'était un village avec une population rurale. Mais qui était le roi de Médina avant l'arrivée de Mahomet? On ne vous en parle pas.

Le même procédé chez moi. Par la suite, nourris de leur théologie musulmane, ils ont commencé à détruire tous les symboles de ce qu'ils appellent le paganisme, et qui n'est pas pour moi du paganisme. Voilà donc comment c'est arrivé.

El Hadj Omar, vous entendez beaucoup parler de lui. Ousmane Dan Fodio, vous entendez beaucoup parler de lui. Ils ont mené une guerre. Et lorsqu'ils sont devenus puissants, vous savez à quoi ils se rattachent en termes de sang de famille? Au prophète Mahomet. Et ils ont créé des écoles, peut-être des civilisations, ils ont apporté des choses, et voilà comment ils se sont installés. Si vous passez du Nigéria vers le Sénégal, vers la Mauritanie, ils ont peut-être quelquefois résisté à la pénétration coloniale, mais la résistance n'avait rien à voir avec la résistance patriotique. C'étaient des conflits religieux. Et que ce soit les Arabes ou les Européens, ils ont pratiqué l'esclavage.

Pour revenir maintenant au temps présent: Que ce soit la religion catholique ou musulmane, nous sommes en train de nous approprier tout cela. Nous avons la croyance très ancrée chez nous, mais peut-être que nous allons avoir une autre pratique.

Nous avons parlé tout à l'heure de langues africaines: Nous avons eu du mal à traduire le Coran en wolof et en poular. Les Perses sont des Musulmans et le Coran est traduit en perse. La pratique se fait en langue persane.

Mais quel est ce dieu qui fait de moi un esclave depuis le Coran et la Bible? Ce dieu je ne veux pas le reconnaître. Si lui pense que je suis esclave, moi je ne le pense pas. Si mes ancêtres ont pratiqué l'esclavage ou en ont été des victimes, j'en souffre. Mais ceux qui continuent à vivre ne seront plus esclaves. Nous mourrons avec la terre. Voilà donc ce qui rend la création très difficile. Ce ne sont pas mes propres principes qui sont en cause. Comment parler en permanence avec mon peuple, comment créer pour mon peuple, pour ne pas les ennuyer pendant deux heures d'écran?

Comme l'a dit Françoise Pfaff, nous n'avons pas inventé les griots. Cela existe dans tous les pays; on a dit les ménestrels. Seulement chez moi le griot était en même temps son propre auteur, son propre musicien, son propre comédien et son propre narrateur. Alors ce qui fait que le griot était important.

Entre tribus, quand il y avait des guerres, on ne tuait jamais le griot. On le tuait seulement quand il mentait. Parce que quand il ment il trompe tout un peuple. Et il avait des devoirs et des droits: Il ne pouvait pas y avoir une assemblée, quelle que soit la société, sans la présence d'un griot. Si le griot représentant n'était pas là, on dit: faites venir son fils. Si le fils n'est pas là, faites venir sa femme, la deuxième, la troisième, la quatrième. Et s'il n'y avait personne dans sa maison, il n'y avait pas de palabre. Voilà donc l'importance du griot pour moi dans ma société.

Cette tradition est devenue caduque et ne peut plus être appliquée. Mais on peut en garder l'esprit, et c'est la façon dont on peut travailler pour être sincère avec les membres de sa société et leur donner conscience.

Voilà toutes les choses qui sont en vrac dans ma tête quand je travaille.

[Which Sudan are you talking about? In Arabic, Sudan designated the country of black people. Which part of Africa do you mean? Northern, Eastern or Western Africa? Wait a minute, I am getting to your question. In West Africa, we situate that period around the tenth century. For Islam to reach Senegal, you have to add about a century. It's very difficult to say how Islam penetrated Africa. It infiltrated very, very slowly. Because, unfortunately, those who are my people—I apologize for using the word "black" for lack of a better word—my ancestors, drawing sustenance from their own culture, were very foolish because they were too generous: They welcomed them, fed them, even gave them wives and let them become hangers-on to the kings who embodied political authority. Unfortunately, like termites, the Muslims did their work from the inside.

You are familiar with the way in which all religions spread, especially Islam. The Arabs give the Hegira as a historical reference. The Hegira is the year Mohammed left Mecca for Medina. Mecca is a real city, Medina was a village with a rural population. But who was the king of Medina before Mohammed came? That nobody talks about.

The same process took place in my country. And after that, imbued with their Muslim theology, they started to destroy all the symbols of what they called paganism, which for me is not paganism, and this is how it came about.

El Hadj Omar, you hear a lot about him, and about Ousmane Dan Fodio as well. They fought a war, and when they became powerful, do you know whom they attached themselves to, in terms of family blood lines? To the prophet Mohammed. The Muslims created schools, perhaps civilizations, they introduced all sorts of objects, and that is how they settled in. If you go from Nigeria to Senegal and to Mauritania, you find that on occasion they may have resisted colonial penetration. However, the resistance had nothing to do with patriotism. It was a religious conflict. And as concerns slavery, they all engaged in it, whether they were Arabs or Europeans.

To return to the present: We are on the way to appropriating both the Catholic and the Muslim religion. Faith is deeply rooted in us, but perhaps we shall practice it differently.

We talked a little while ago about African languages: We found it very difficult to translate the Koran into Wolof and Poular, while the Persian people are Muslim and the Koran has been translated into Persian. They worship in Persian.

But what kind of a God is this who has made a slave of me from the time of the Koran and the Bible? Such a God I do not want to recognize. If that God thinks I am a slave, I do not agree. If my ancestors practiced slavery or were slaves, that grieves me. But those who are living now shall not be slaves. We will die fighting for the land. That is what makes it very difficult to create a work of art. It is not my own principles which are at issue, but the problem of maintaining a continuous dialogue with my people, of creating for my people so as not to bore them for two hours.

As Françoise Pfaff said, we did not invent the griots. They exist in every country: people talk of minstrels. But in my country the griot was at one and the same time his own author, his own musician, his own actor, and his own narrator. This made the griot a very important person, despite the fact that, according to general opinion, we were barbarians and savages.

When there were wars between different tribes, griots were never killed. The griot would only be killed when he was lying. Because when the griot lies he deceives an entire people. The griot also had duties and rights: no assembly could be held without the presence of a griot, whatever the social group. If the representative griot was absent, people said: "Call his son; if the son is not there, call his wife—the second, the third, the fourth." And if there was nobody in his house, no meeting took place. That is for me the importance of the griot in my society.

This tradition is out of date and can no longer be applied today. But its spirit can be preserved. That is how one can work and be sincere with one's own society and make people aware of their situation.

I have given you the thoughts that run through my head, in no particular order, when I am working.]

PART TWO

WRITERS' FORUM:
LANGUAGE AND THE WRITER

The afternoon session of the conference was conceived as a public conversation in which writers from Africa, the Caribbean, and the United States would explore topics, problems, and experiences they shared as writers, using Sembène's work as a point of departure. Unlike many such round-tables, where the participants know each other and re-enact in public the discussions they have already held in private or in print, this forum was unrehearsed. Some of the writers had never met each other before.[50] On the evening before the conference, the writers gathered at the home of Rhonda Cobham-Sander and Reinhard Sander to discuss the themes they would develop the next day. They were joined by Samba Gadjigo, Thomas Cassirer, and Michael Thelwell.

The writers decided to focus their discussion on language, and from that point of reference to develop several ideas. On the one hand, they wanted to discuss the technical issues of expression, editing, and publication that they face. At the same time, they wanted to stress that to *write* a language and then to have it read is a political act of cultural legitimation in a world where majoritarian forces are at work to shrink the universe of written languages, a theme most notably developed in Ngugi wa Thiong'o's collection of essays, *Decolonising the Mind: The Politics of Language in African Literature*. As writers they wanted to highlight that language is a striking metaphor for voice, role, self-knowledge, praxis, and personal power. Furthermore, these writers of African ancestry saw in their appropriation of colonial European languages a poignant expression of the contradictions of contemporary cultural politics and the ambiguity—structured by race, class, and imperialism—of their own positions within this discourse.

In the unrehearsed discussion that follows, each writer—with the exception of Sembène—makes a brief statement; then they discuss each other's ideas and respond to questions from the audience, with Samba Gadjigo playing the role of moderator. Self-criticism and personal integrity, the deconstruction of dominant representations of the past and present, and the assertion, even the demand, that African and diaspora voices be heard and reckoned with are not only important ideas in Africa and throughout the African diaspora, but they are essential ingredients in any counter-hegemonic practice.

Toni Cade Bambara

I want to talk about language, form, and changing the world. The question that faces billions of people at this moment, one decade shy of the twenty-first century is: Can the planet be rescued from the psychopaths? The persistent concern of engaged artists, of cultural workers, in this country, and certainly within my community, is what role can, should, or must the film practitioner, for example, play in producing a desirable vision of the future? And the challenge that the cultural worker faces, myself for example, as a writer and as a media activist, is that the tools of my trade are colonized. The creative imagination has been colonized. The global screen has been colonized. And the audience—readers and viewers—is in bondage to an industry. It has the money, the will, the muscle, and the propaganda machine oiled up to keep us all locked up in a delusional system—as to even what America is. We are taught to believe, for example, that there is an American literature, that there is an American cinema, that there is an American reality.

There is no American literature; there are American literatures. There are those who have their roots in the most ancient civilizations—African, Asian, or Mexican— and there are those that have the most ancient roots in this place, that mouth-to-ear tradition of the indigenous peoples that were here thousands and thousands of years before it was called America, thousands of years before it was even called Turtle Island. And there is too the literature of the European settlement regime that calls itself American literature.

There is no American cinema; there are American cinemas. There is the conventional cinema that masks its ideological imperatives as entertainment and normalizes its hegemony with the term "convention," that is to say the cinematic practices—of editing, particular uses of narrative structure, the development of genres, the language of spatial relationships, particular performatory styles of act- ing—are called conventions because they are represented somehow to be transcendent or universal, when in fact these practices are based on a history of imperialism and violence—the violent suppression of any other production of cinematic practices. Eduardo Galeano, the Latin American writer and cultural critic, speaking to this issue of convention and imperialism, once remarked that if Hemingway had been born in Turkey the world would never have heard of Hemingway. That is to say, the greatness of a writer or the greatness of any cultural production is determined by the power of that writer's country.

So there is the commercial cinema; there is also in this country the independent cinema or new American cinema or the new alternative American cinema, and it's being advanced by practitioners, theoreticians, programmers, and supporters of various cultural communities: the African American community, the native American community, the American Latino community, the Pacific rim and American Asian community, and the American European community. And they insist on, or rather by their very existence challenge, the notion that there is only one way to make a film: Hollywood style; that there are only two motives for making films: entertainment and profit; and that there is only one set of critical criteria for evaluating these products. Within that movement there is an alternative wing in this country that is devoted to the notion of socially responsible cinema, that is interested in exploring the potential of cinema for social transformation, and these practitioners continue to struggle to tell the American story. That involves assuming the enormous tasks of reconstructing cultural memory, of revitalizing usable traditions of cultural practices, and of resisting the wholesale and unacknowledged appropriation of cultural items—such as music, language style, posture—by the industry that then attempts to suppress the roots of it— where it came from—in order to sustain its ideological hegemony. And so, there is no single American reality. There are versions, perspectives, that are specific to the historical experiences and cultural heritages of various communities in this country.

Many contemporary independent filmmakers were provoked into picking up the camera and trying to devise filmic equivalents for our cultural and social and political discourse as a result of their encounters with the guardians of English language purity. That is to say, they were moved by the terrorism—systematic, random, institutional, and personal—of those thugs who would have youngsters going through their educational careers believing that they need remedial English, that the language they speak at home may be okay for home but in the real world they are going to have to learn standard English in order to participate in this society. Many of the independent filmmakers have been hearing all their lives that you can't speak Spanish on school grounds, what you're speaking is not standard, is not appropriate, or you Chinese people have got to learn how to speak up and stop squeaking.

Before we get to the issue of what idiom should one speak in, there is the prior struggle of who may speak. The normalization of the term minority—for people who are not white, male, bourgeois, and Christian—is a treacherous one. The term, which has an operational role in the whole politics of silence, invisibility, and amnesia, comes from the legal arena. It says that a minority or a minor may not give testimony in court without an advocate, without a go-between, without a mediating something or other, without a professional mouthpiece, without someone monitoring the speak- ing and the tongue—which is one of the many reasons I do not use the term "minority" for anybody, most especially not myself. The second question is what will be the nature of the tongue? The independent filmmaker, who may not have any particular political agenda, who may not even have coherent politics but simply wishes to tell a story, discovers all too soon that the very conventions—the very tools, practices—in which that filmmaker has been trained were not designed to accommodate her or his story, her or his people, her or his cultural heritage, her or his issues, and that filmmaker will then face a choice: either to devise a new film language in order to get that story told or to have the whole enterprise derailed by those conventions.

If time were to permit it, I would look at the career of Luis Valdez, looking at two films, "La Bamba" and "Zoot Suit," the first made for so-called cross-over audiences while the second was made for his authenticating audience: the Chicano community. So we can see the difference in film language, the difference in film practices. But we'll jump over that.

The importance of Sembène, as a practitioner, is an occasion for twenty-five years of film talk throughout the African diaspora, indeed throughout world film culture. And Sembène as an exemplary model of persistence and insistence on cultural integrity is at the moment immeasurable. So I'll jump over that and simply call attention to the language of space in Sembène's work. In Hollywood, space is hidden as a rule. For a more cogent, comprehensive and coherent version of what I'm getting ready to say, I would refer you to an interview conducted in Ouagadougou at the Pan-African film festival in 1989 with Sembène by Manthia Diawara, the African cinema theorist, but here is the short drift: In Hollywood space is hidden. Once you get an establishing shot—Chicago skyline, night, winter—most of the other shots are tight shots. We move up on the speaker, we then shift for a reaction shot, tight space, and the spectator is supposed to do the work and figure out what is happening outside of the frame. But for a people concerned with land, with turf, with real estate, with home, with the whole colonial experience, with the appropriation of space by the elite or by the outsider, the language of space becomes very crucial within the cinematic practice. In "Mandabi," recall the women in their space: the shadows from the building, the sun, the legs stretched out, the calabashes. We don't have to work to invent or re-create contiguous reality; we are very aware of the space, so that when someone intrudes and messes it all up, a tremendous statement is getting made that resonates historically.

In "Ceddo," in the re-creation of seventeenth-century Wolof society, we don't get any tight shots because we are very much concerned here with the whole history of the appropriation of space. The king and the spokesman have their space, the imam on the blanket has his space, his people around him have their space. The princess and the *ceddo* are in a particular space, and he even throws a rope on the ground and says, "You stay on that side of the space or I will cut your throat." The Christian missionary is in his space. And then there is the space of future time: the fast-forward space. Further, there's the space when people are being hemmed up, shaved, renamed, and are about to undergo this traumatic experience. Just in front of the hemmed-up folks is a space that Sembène leaves vacant. In a non-African film that space would be taken up with pictures and actions, namely the affixing of shackles and chains, the building of fires, and the use of branding irons to explain what is going to happen. Sembène leaves that space vacant and moves to the soundtrack. And on the soundtrack we get African-American music; we get spirituals to tell that story that will take place in another space. It's not Wolof music; it's not African music—that's from that other space. Rather, it's African-American music—a moment of diasporic hookup.

Earl Lovelace

I want first of all to introduce myself and to comment on the subject which we have at hand: the dialectics of form and content. What I propose to do by way of introduction is to read from a novel that I have written, then perhaps speak for five minutes or so about some ideas that I have in relation to my writing, expecting of course that the writing that I read would more properly express me than what I have subsequently to say. This is taken from *The Dragon Can't Dance* and this is the prologue and it's called "The Hill."

> This is the hill tall above the city where Taffy, a man who say he is Christ, put himself up on a cross one burning midday and say to his followers: 'Crucify me! Let me die for my people. Stone me with stones as you stone Jesus, I will love you still.' And when they start to stone him in truth he get vex and start to cuss: 'Get me down! Get me down!' he say. 'Let every sinnerman bear his own blasted burden; who is I to die for people who ain't have sense enough to know that they can't pelt a man with big stones when so much little pebbles lying on the ground.'

> This is the hill, Calvary Hill, where the sun set on starvation and rise on potholed roads, thrones for stray dogs that you could play banjo on their rib bones, holding garbage piled high like a cathedral spire, sparkling with flies buzzing like torpedoes; and if you want to pass from your yard to the road you have to be a high-jumper to jump over the gutter full up with dirty water, and hold your nose. Is noise whole day. Laughter is not laughter; it is a groan coming from the bosom of these houses—no—not houses, shacks that leap out of the red dirt and stone, thin like smoke, fragile like kite paper, balancing on their rickety pillars as broomsticks on the edge of a juggler's nose.

> This is the hill, swelling and curling like a machauel snake from Observatory Street to the mango fields in the back of Morvant, its guts stretched to bursting with a thousand narrow streets and alleys and lanes and traces and holes, holding the people who come on the edge of this city to make it home.

> This hill is it; and in it; in Alice Street, named for Princess Alice, the Queen's aunt—Alice—soft word on the lips, is a yard before which grows a governor plum tree that has battled its way up through the tough red dirt and stands now, its roots spread out like claws, gripping the earth, its leaves rust red and green, a bouquet in this desert place. . .[51]

I have read this extract to demonstrate that the language I employ not only locates me, but expresses me. That is to say it tells that I come from a place in the world and that I come out of a particular experience. It is that experience I see myself as a writer struggling to wrestle into language and by that means bring it into the world. In a way there is nothing remarkable about that because I believe every individual writer must have his or her own experience, and seeks to wrestle that experience into language and to bring it into the world. In a way I believe that the task I have is the task of every individual writer, but also I think that because our history is not so well known—but we have some sense of its outlines—and because my experience as part of a community that has not been properly represented in the language of the world, the task is all the more compelling.

Representations by others have not been adequate either for the people ourselves or for the others who view us and who have to deal with them and have to deal with us. It is I who must bring this language and experience into the world. What is that experience? I believe that it is important to give some kind of sense of that experience, as a Caribbean person as well as a person in the world, but I am speaking as a Caribbean person for the moment. I think that our experience has had as its central theme not slavery and colonialism, as is often thought, but the struggle against enslavement and colonialism. I want to repeat that our experience is not an experience of slavery and colonialism, but our experience is the experience of the struggle against enslavement and colonialism. In that process we have needed to affirm the self, to have some sense of moral order, some sense of justice, some sense of what it is to be human, and I think it is principally an experience of struggle that we bring to the world. Hopefully, I think that the bringing of that experience into language and presenting it into the world could change the world. I say that as a writer my own struggle is to wrestle that language into the world, also to be present in the world and to claim the struggling experience in the world as well. You know, this world doesn't belong to somebody else and it doesn't belong to just me either. It belongs to me too. I say that sets the terms of my writing: I deal not particularly with a little group of people somewhere on the periphery of existence, but at the very center of existence.

Ngugi wa Thiong'o

It would make my task easier if I could begin and end my speech by saying that I absolutely agree with everything that has been said by the two previous speakers. The themes they have isolated for discussion are pertinent to this particular panel and also to our entire enterprise as writers of African origins who now inhabit all the corners of the world. It is important that we are having this discussion in the context of the work of Ousmane Sembène. When I read his work or come to his films, one of the questions which I find fairly central is that of language. Even in his earliest work he tried to address the question of language—not only language as a system of signs, but also language in the larger context of social struggle.

I was thinking about this panel two days ago when one of the students in my class at Yale told me that she was going to watch a film on Kenya called "Kitchen Toto," and she invited me to see the film on video along with one or two others from Kenya. The issues arising from that film are pertinent to the whole question of language. For those of you who have not seen that particular film, it opens with shots of Kenyan colonial settlers playing with African children in a school context. So the opening shot of the film shows the colonial settler clearly in harmony with Kenyan African children. There follows a sequence of shots of a good Christian African and these shots are such that we are placed in a very sympathetic relationship to him. We are also shown stills of the African Christian priest with his family. Our eyes focus on that particular family. Later we see him in a church preaching against the evil that has come to the land. Into this very sympathetic family—Christian, African, obedient to the West and so on— come Mau Mau terrorists. They come with their machetes and they hack the good Christian African family into pieces. No explanation is given as to why they are doing it; it's just an act of sheer brutality. So no matter what the film says afterwards about the struggle between the two polarities of white racism and African resistance, we are already against these Mau Mau terrorists. In the same film the colonial state as represented by the good white policeman becomes the arbiter in a kind of semi-civil war between extremist whites and, I presume, also equally extremist actors in the resistance. So at the end of the film, in a sense, we are shown that a colonial state is really a liberal state. It is a liberal referee in a system of civil war. In the film the African people involved in resistance have been denied a voice. They do not even have a language, for the language which they speak—even when they are peasants and workers—is good King's or Queen's English. It is as if the Mau Mau resistance forces did not really have a language of their own.

Now this denial of the voice to those who resist is fairly central to the literary consciousness in the West which on the whole has been in harmony with the forces of imperialist domination of other countries. I want to illustrate this gradual denial of the voice to those who resist by mentioning just a couple of texts which you will all recognize. And these texts cover the whole historical period of this domination of the rest of the world by a handful of European nations.

The first text is Shakespeare's *The Tempest*. And you remember there that Caliban, whose island has been taken over by Prospero, is represented as having no language although we presume that before Prospero came to the island Caliban had been speaking to his mother in a certain language. But in the play he has no language of his own. However, it is very interesting that Shakespeare, after he has given him the English language, at least makes Caliban have a voice even though this voice is in the English language.

We come to another text, Defoe's *Robinson Crusoe*. And you remember the contact between Friday and Crusoe: Crusoe here meets Friday and begins to teach him a language. Again we perceive that Friday is presumed to have no language. He is being given a language. And the first thing he is told is, "Your name is Friday." Then he is told to say, "Master, Master," and then he is told, "that is my name." "Your name is Friday; my name is Master." It is again interesting that Defoe was quite satiric about this whole encounter. Friday has some kind of voice for he does, or he is made to, doubt Crusoe's conception of the origins of the world in the divine order. But still, Friday has much less of a voice than Caliban.

We come to the twentieth century, to Joseph Conrad's *Heart of Darkness*, a text which is in so many ways consistently against colonial adventurism. It paints colonial adventurism in very strong negative colors. Nevertheless, the African people there have absolutely no voice. This time they don't have a language. And one of only two sentences Africans are given is: "Mistah Kurtz—he dead." Otherwise, they are seen as merging with the shadows and the darkness. They are part of the gloom.

Now, I want to mention a fourth text—this time from South Africa. It is written by a novelist who is right now very much celebrated in the West: J. M. Coetzee. And he has rendered, or he has told, Friday's story under the title *Foe*. And here in the midst of South Africa, where you would think that the retelling of the story would make an entirely different statement, here Friday's/Caliban's tongue has been pulled out. So there is not even a pretense that he has a tongue, a physical tongue with which he can speak.

I mention these cases because the whole enterprise of writers on the African continent—and in many ways symbolized by Ousmane Sembène—has been to give voice to those forces which have been struggling over the centuries to regain their voice, to regain their language. In other words, to regain their space in the twentieth century. Now, as these writers give voice to those forces which have been trying to reclaim their voices and their languages, they are, in so many ways, the central literary voices of the twentieth century. For the twentieth century is in effect a creation of two traditions. One is the imperialist—the colonial—tradition with its roots in slavery, slave trade, classical colonialism, and to today's transnational type of neo-colonialism—the one which is also connected with those forces described by Toni as "psychopaths who are trying to ruin the world." The other tradition is the tradition of resistance against slavery, against classical colonialism, against today's various forms of colonial control, and various other forms of domination.

So as we move towards the twenty-first century, we can say that those forces which are part of the struggle against enslavement and colonialism are the makers of the twentieth century. The neglect of this crucial resistance tradition in studies in various universities of the world is really a neglect of voices which are not marginal to the twentieth century, but voices which are central to the twentieth century and to the making of a new tomorrow in the world. I'm glad that these voices are so ably represented here, more so in the work of Ousmane Sembène in both literature and film.

John Wideman

I'd like to call your attention to the fact that this is Saturday afternoon in the good ole
U. S. of A., and that in cities all over this country, and in some small towns also, there
will be many young black men waking up with knots upside their heads, with a terrible
drug or alcohol hangover, with charges against them that are going to influence and
destroy the rest of their lives, and you won't hear them talking; they don't have a voice.
That's why I'm reminding you of their predicament this Saturday. And in some futile
gesture, I'll dedicate these remarks to that particular group of voiceless people. And
the other side of that is this: there will be many black women waking up in this country
who are connected to those men in intimate ways, and their lives will be suffering a
blight as well.

In my fiction, I work with language all the time, and I'm going to speak rather
narrowly about language now. Since we're treated as marginal—politically, economically, and culturally—African-American writers have a special vexing stake in
reforming, revitalizing the American imagination. History is a cage, a conundrum we
must escape or resolve before our art can go freely about its business. As has always
been the case in order to break into print, we must be prepared to deal with the extra-
literary forces that have conspired to keep us silent; for our stories, novels, and poems
will continue to be treated just as marginally as our lives. Editors know that their jobs
depend upon purveying images the public recognizes and approves, so they resist our
fictions and almost never choose those which transcend stereotypes and threaten to
expose the fantasies of superiority, the bedrock lies and brute force that sustain the
majority's power over the "other." Framed in foreign inimicable contexts, our stories
appear at best as exotic slices of life and local color, at worst as ghettoized irrelevan-
cies. However, as Sembène reminds us, the battle for acceptance into the European-
American mainstream must not obscure our primary responsibility to express ourselves fully, truly, to ourselves, and to the generations that follow. We must both invent
and achieve an audience—the audience of fathers, mothers, sisters, brothers, and
children who share with us and need the alphabet of African-derived cultures. When
we remember our roots—the social conditions, slavery, oppression, marginality, and
the expressive resources we employ to cope with these conditions, the counter-reality
we elaborate through art—when we don't allow ourselves to be distracted, that is, we
keep telling the truth which brought us into being—when we remember the necessity
of remaining human, defining human in our own terms, resisting those destructive
definitions in the master's tongue, attitudes, and art, then our tradition remains alive,
a referent, a repository of value, money we can take to the bank.

Afro-American traditions contain the memory of a hard unclean break with the

African past. This partially accounts for key postures that are subversive, disruptive, disjunctive. To the brutality that once ripped us away and now tries to rip us apart, we turn a stylized mask of indifference, of malleability, a core of iron silent refusal while our feet, **feet**, *feet* dance to another beat. I look for and cherish this in our fiction.

Is there any difference between sitting in at an all-white lunch counter and an African-American writer composing a story in English? What's the fate of a black story in a white world of white stories? How do we break out of the dangerous circle of majority-controlled publishing houses, distributors, critics, editors, readers, and reconnect with our primary audience? Vernacular language is not enough. Integration is not enough. If what a writer wants is freedom of expression, then somehow that larger goal must be addressed implicitly and explicitly in our fiction. A story should contain clues that align it with tradition and critique traditions, that establish the new space it requires, demands, appropriates, and that hint at how it may bring forth other things like itself where these others have, will, and are coming from. This does not mean defining criteria for admitting stories into some ideologically sound privileged category, but seeking conditions that maximize the possibility of free, original expression. We must continue inventing our stories—our lives—expressing, not sacrificing, the double and triple African consciousness that is our heritage.

Black music illuminates the glories and pitfalls, the possibility of integrity, how artists nourished by shared cultural roots can prove again and again that even though they are moving through raindrops, they don't have to get soaked. Their art signifies they are in the storm, but not of it. Black music is a moveable feast, wedded to modern technology. It illustrates the power of African-derived art to change the world. What lessons are transferable to the realm of literature? Is musical language freer, less inscribed with the historical baggage of European hegemony, exploitation, racism? Is it practical within the forms and frequencies of this instrument—written English—to roll back history, those negative accretions, those iron bars, and "White Only" signs that steal one's voice, one's breath away? Our fiction can express the dialectic, the tension, the conversation, the warfare of competing versions of reality the English language contains. One crucial first step may be recognizing that African/European, black/white, either/or perceptions of the tensions within language are woefully inadequate. Start by taking nothing for granted, giving nothing away. Study the language, the way our historians have begun to comb the past. Contest, contest. Return junk mail to sender. Call into question the language's complacencies about itself. At the level of spelling and grammar, how language is taught to our children, but also deeper, its sounds. Decode its coded pretensions to legitimacy, gentility, exclusivity, seniority, logic. Unveil chaos within the patterns of certainty. Restate issues and paradigms so they are not simply the old race problem relexified. Whose language is this, anyway?

Martin Bernal, in *Black Athena*, has traced the link between European theories of race and language, how 19th-century models of language development parallel, buttress, and reinforce hierarchical concepts of race and culture—the same text we're using now. He examines how social sciences—the soft core posing as the hard core of academic humanities curricula—were tainted at their inception by racist assumptions and agendas, how romantic linguistic theory was used as a tool to "prove" the superiority of the West. And he shows how uncritical absorption of certain hallowed tenets of western thought is like participating in your own lynching. Be prepared to critique any call for back-to-basics in light of the research Bernal gathers and summarizes. The great lie that systems of thought are pure, universal, uncontaminated by cultural bias continues to be brought forth by the "killer B's"—people like Bush and Bennett—for public consumption. Whose great books—in whose interests—must be read? Whose stories should be told? By whom? To what ends?

Language grows and changes; we should study the dynamics that allow individual speakers to learn a language, to adapt it to the infinite geography of their inner imaginative worlds and of their outer social play, as well as the constant intercourse of both. The writer can love language and also keep it at arm's length as a medium, foregrounding its arbitrariness, its treacherousness, never calling it his/her own, never completely identifying with it, but making intimate claims by exploring what it can do, what it could do, if the writer has patience, luck, skill and practices, **practices**, *practices*. In it, but not of it, and that stance produces bodies of enabling legislation, a grammar of nuanced tensions, incompatibilities, opens doors and windows that not only dramatize the stance itself, but implicate the medium. This language I'm using constantly pulls in many directions at once, and unless we keep alert, keep fighting the undertow, acknowledge the currents going my way and every other damn way, I drown. I'm not alone but not separate either. Any voice I accomplish is really many voices, and the most powerful voices are always steeped in unutterable silences, the silences of our ancestors, and children denied a voice in this land. A story is a formula for extracting meaning from chaos, a handful of water we scoop up to recall an ocean. We need readers who are willing to be co-conspirators. It's at this level of primal encounter that we must operate in order to reclaim the language. The hidden subjects are always: what are we saying when we use this language? Where does it come from? Where do I come from? Where do we meet and how shall I name this meeting place? What is food? What is eating? Why do people go to lunch counters? Black music offers a counter-integrative model because it poses fundamental questions about music and fills us with the thrill of knowing yes, *yes* the answers and the questions are still up for grabs, and my, **my** answers and questions count at least as much—and maybe more—than anyone else's.

Ousmane Sembène

J'ai écouté avec beaucoup d'attention et de plaisir ces différents propos raccourcis qui, j'en suis sûr, n'expriment pas totalement la forme et le sens des pensées des participants. Et ce qu'ils gardent pour eux est encore plus riche que ce qu'ils nous ont dit. Nous espérons pouvoir bénéficier, par un bref survol, de ce qui a été dit.

Ngugi l'a rappelé: Nous tous venons de différents coins du monde, mais nous avons la même racine, c'est l'Afrique. Nous exprimons des civilisations et des situations différentes, mais nous avons un même métier et un même désir. Ngugi est l'ennemi de son gouvernement. Ce n'est pas lui qui est l'adversaire, c'est son gouvernement qui est son adversaire. Et Ngugi n'est pas l'adversaire de son peuple, il veut la richesse de son pays. Chaque fois que je le rencontre j'ai les larmes aux yeux.

Dans l'ensemble de l'Afrique, depuis l'indépendance, il y a à peu près trente ans, les nouveaux bourgeois africains ont tué plus de cadres intellectuels africains que cent ans de colonisation, ou alors ils les ont poussés à l'exil, jusqu'à leur périssement mental. C'est pour vous dire donc que chaque fois que Ngugi aborde un sujet, pour lui c'est sa vie.

Je viens du Sénégal, où la tolérance est plus poussée. Je ne le dois pas à mon gouvernement, je le dois à mon peuple, et je le dois aussi à vous tous à travers le monde. Je me souviens, un jour, des universitaires sont venus me voir, chez moi, et ils m'ont dit: "Ils ont arrêté ton ami et frère, Ngugi, au Kenya; qu'est-ce que nous devons faire?" Dans la nuit nous avons fait des télégrammes, nous les avons envoyés, et chaque télégramme était doublé, il était envoyé au destinataire et aussi au gouvernement sénégalais.

Quand, quelque temps après, j'ai eu l'occasion de voir Senghor, qui était à l'époque président de la république, il m'a dit: "Mais tu passes toujours ton temps à protester, pourquoi ne pas t'occuper seulement de toi?" Et je lui ai répondu, par voie de presse, que seul, je ne représente absolument rien et je ne sers à rien du tout. Quand quelque chose se passe aux Caraïbes et que nous sommes saisis, nous essayons d'agir, de faire comprendre. Quand quelque chose se passe aux Etats-Unis, nous essayons de faire la même chose. Nous sommes des leaders d'opinion avec des pouvoirs d'action limités dans l'immédiat, mais à long terme nous voyons des résultats. Je vous explique cela seulement pour vous montrer que le travail que nous faisons n'est pas à minimiser.

Je demande toujours à mon peuple, au peuple africain: "Pourquoi avez vous besoin d'artistes, je n'ai pas dit de bâtisseurs mais de créateurs, de musiciens, d'écrivains et de peintres?" Vous-mêmes vous pouvez y réfléchir: Qu'est-ce que vous attendez de nous?

Nous autres artistes, nous pouvons vous dire ce que nous attendons de vous: le sens de la justice, l'équité. Vous-mêmes, vous vous assumez en disant que tous les hommes sont égaux et ont une culture. Il n'y a pas de grande ou de petite culture. Comme les doigts de la main, tous les cinq sont utiles. Ce n'est pas la longueur d'un doigt qui fait une main.

Revenons seulement sur cette leçon de liberté. Quand j'ai fait "Ceddo," mon ami Soyinka a vu le film aux Etats-Unis. On lui a demandé ce qu'il en pensait, et il a dit qu'il l'aurait interdit. Il n'avait pas alors le prix Nobel de littérature. Il a eu le Nobel et nous en sommes très fiers. Quand il y a eu le problème du livre de Rushdie, au Nigéria Soyinka a pris position pour Rushdie, au nom de la liberté. Les imams du Nigéria l'ont sommé de se taire et de se désolidariser avec Rushdie. Quand je l'ai vu je lui ai dit : "Si tu ne tues pas l'imam, si ta femme ne tue pas l'imam, c'est l'imam qui te tue." C'est la leçon de la liberté. Donc la liberté n'est pas unilatérale, ce n'est pas vers l'Europe seulement. Voilà l'aspect qui est encore intéressant dans notre débat.

Venons-en à la question des langues africaines. Pendant longtemps on a pensé que c'étaient des dialectes, que l'Afrique n'avait pas de culture. Maintenant nous avons dépassé cela, bien qu'il en reste encore des résidus dans la tête de certains universitaires et académiciens. Mais ce n'est pas grave. Ce qui est grave, c'est que ceux qui nous gouvernent, les gouvernements africains eux-mêmes, n'ont pas le courage de considérer que la langue est un élément de nourriture culturelle et économique. Il ne s'agit pas de penser que le gikuyu est une langue riche. C'est une langue comme le masaï, comme le wolof et les autres langues. Voilà le combat que nous avons à mener chez nous-mêmes d'abord, avant de le mener aux Etats-Unis ou en Europe.

Peut-être que je vais être un mauvais prophète pour les Etats-Unis, mais je sais qu'il y a beaucoup d'Afro-Américains qui apprennent le swahili, le bambara ou le peul. Vous pouvez noter que dans les quinze ans à venir, nous aurons des Afro-Américains qui vont parler les langues africaines. Cela ne veut pas dire qu'ils vont rejeter l'anglais, le français, le chinois ou le polonais. Mais cela sera leur langue de communication, comme l'Italien a sa langue ici, comme le yiddish ou l'espagnol. En attendant, je m'arrête là pour permettre aux autres de parler.

[I have listened with great attention and pleasure to these different statements, but in a summarized form. I am sure these statements do not express completely the form and the sense of the thinking of the panel participants, and what they have kept back is even richer than what they told us. We hope to benefit by a quick overview of what has been said.

Ngugi has reminded us that we all come from different corners of the world but have the same roots in Africa. We give expression to different civilizations and situations, but we have the same profession and the same objective. Ngugi, in particular, is the enemy of his government. It is not he who is the adversary, it is

Ngugi's government that is his adversary. Nor is Ngugi the adversary of his people, he wants his country to be prosperous. Every time I meet him tears come to my eyes.

In the whole of Africa since independence, some thirty years ago, the new African *bourgeoisie* has killed more African intellectuals than did one hundred years of colonialism, or else they have driven them into exile until, intellectually, they are destroyed. This is to let you know that whenever Ngugi takes up a topic, it is his life that is at issue.

I come from Senegal where there is more tolerance. This I owe not to my government, but to my people. I owe it also to all of you throughout the world. I remember the day when some academics came to see me at my house, and said: "Your friend and brother Ngugi has been arrested in Kenya, what shall we do?" That night we drew up telegrams and we sent them off. All the telegrams were sent in duplicate, one copy to the addressee, and the other to the Senegalese government.

Some time after that I had the opportunity to meet Senghor who was then the president of Senegal. He told me: "Why is it that you spend all your time protesting, why don't you just mind your own business?" I answered him through the media, that by myself I do not represent anything at all and am of no use whatsoever. When something happens in the Antilles and we are called upon, we try to take action and make people understand what is going on. When something is happening in the United States we try to do the same. We are opinion leaders with limited capacity for immediate action. But in the long run, we see results. I am giving this explanation only to let you see that the work we do should not be belittled.

I always ask my people, the African people: "Why do you need artists? I'm not talking about builders, but creative individuals, musicians, writers, and painters." You in the audience might also think about what you expect of us.

As for us, we can tell you what we expect from you: a sense of justice and fairness. You take on responsibility for yourselves when you say that all human beings are equal and have their own culture. There is no culture that is great or insignificant. As with the fingers of the hand, all five are useful. It's not the length of a finger that makes the hand a hand.

To come back to this notion of liberty: When I made "Ceddo," my friend Soyinka saw the film in the United States. He was asked what he thought of it and he said he would have forbidden the film to be shown. At that moment, he had not yet received the Nobel prize in literature. He did receive the Nobel prize and we are really proud of that. There was also the Salman Rushdie affair. In Nigeria Soyinka came out in favor of Rushdie, in the name of liberty. The imams of Nigeria told him not to speak out and not to show solidarity with Rushdie. When I saw him, I told him: "If you don't kill the imam and if your wife doesn't kill him, it's the imam who will kill you." That is the lesson that freedom teaches us: Liberty is not unilateral. It does not merely mean freedom from European domination. That is another interesting aspect of our discussion.

Let us turn to the question of African languages. They were long considered dialects and it was said that Africa had no culture. Now we have gone beyond that, even though the notion still remains in the heads of certain academics. But that is not a serious problem. What is alarming is that those who govern us, the African governments, do not have the courage to consider that language sustains culture and the economy. What matters is not to think of Gikuyu as a rich language. It is a language like Masaï, Wolof and other languages. This is the struggle we have to fight back home before we even start carrying it into Europe or the United States.

Perhaps I am going to be a bad prophet for the United States, but I know that there are many African Americans who learn Swahili, Peul or Bambara. You can be sure that in fifteen years we will have African Americans speaking African languages. That does not mean that they are going to reject English, French, Chinese, or Polish. But the African language will be their language of communication, just as the Italians still have their language in America, or like Yiddish or Spanish. I am going to stop here to allow others to speak.]

Discussion Among the Writers

Samba Gadjigo: In many ways you have obliquely touched on this; but I'd like to see you address it explicitly: To what extent do race, class, and gender—but especially race—interfere with, affect, or inform the production and reception of artistic works?

Toni Cade Bambara: Thank you for the question. I thought that's what we were addressing among other things. Of course, it matters; it's one of those crucial issues about which there cannot be silence. The official version on those issues has to be challenged. Take the film "Sidewalk Stories" by Charles Lane: independent film, black and white, less than a $300,000 budget, twelve-minute standing ovation at the Cannes Film Festival, a product of the independent black cinema. What can happen when you do your script, you go into production, you're through with post-production, and you haven't really run it through a race, class, gender analysis before you finish editing. I pick "Sidewalk Stories" because I think it is well thought out, it's not exploitative, it doesn't hustle working-class poor people in its depiction of the homeless milieu. It's very careful and concerned in its depiction and its representation of black women in the film. But there is a moment in the shelter when the sidewalk artist with the young girl—the little kid that he has rescued—wants to make sure he doesn't lose track of her. So he ties a little string around her foot and a little string around her wrist and then he ties it around his neck. This image, this gesture, this bit comes from a Chaplin film; in fact, we see it in a great many of the early European-American films. But that image of a black man with a rope around his neck begins to disrupt and derail the film for just a moment. In other words, the comedy of that scene doesn't come off, certainly not for black spectators. There is too much baggage around that picture for that scene to come off. It's one example in the whole film that I have any problem with because this is an unusually careful film in terms of addressing issues of race, class, and gender.

Earl Lovelace: Does race or class matter? Matter to the writer? To the viewer? As a writer you don't see the reader, so I suppose it really wouldn't matter. But I suppose that writing in the world, you'd expect there would be both white people and black people or anybody and everybody, hopefully. Certainly, I would want to think that for my own writing. I would want to relate in a particular kind of way to black people, given our history and given the fact that we have been so poorly represented, and hopefully I would be saying something that would help in some kind of way.

Ngugi wa Thiong'o: I agree with that. I think the problem is that people are not really understanding the question, but they know what has been said. In the whole discussion of all the panelists today, we have assumed the interplay of race, class, and gender. There is no way you can isolate any sensibility in today's world which has not been affected by the interplay of race, class, and gender. If you take the 400-500 years of imperialist domination from its origins in Renaissance Europe to the present—if you talk about slavery and the slave trade—it's a certain category of people of a certain race, of a certain class enslaving people of a certain category of race, class, and so on. And even within that category, the issue of gender in terms of say how different groups were affected, the gender question was also very much central to that. So, there's no way to ignore it, because it's impossible to ignore the interplay of those three: race, class, and gender. And in fact in this case they are so pertinent to Ousmane Sembène's work, whether you're taking *God's Bits of Wood*, or for that matter the last novel, *The Last of the Empire*, what is interesting is the way the various conflicts among the various characters are very much rooted in those issues of race, class, and gender. And in some ways, there is no better way of answering that question than actually to refer to aspects of the work of Ousmane Sembène.

Ousmane Sembène: *Pour ma part, je voulais seulement apporter un petit détail. Peut-être que la conception que j'ai des blancs dans ma tête diffère de celle de mes frères et soeurs de l'Amérique qui sont dans des ghettos. Peut-être qu'ils sont les plus étouffés par les Européens. Etant donné que moi, j'ai ma culture, ma langue, j'ai un repli sur moi-même: ce que j'appelle mes valeurs de refuge. De ce fait, quand je revendique, je dis: il est étranger sur ma terre. Et si je prends ce que je sais de la littérature afro-américaine depuis Du Bois jusqu'à nos jours, jusqu'à Toni Cade Bambara, les situations diffèrent. Mais, de toute façon, je pense que le problème est très délicat. Nous le posons.*

Maintenant, en 1990, il y a des drapeaux, des hymnes, des gouvernements africains. C'est l'époque du néo-colonialisme. J'ai mon gouvernement noir, malgré qu'il soit mauvais, capitaliste, bourgeois, et manipulé par le néo-colonialisme. Après l'indépendance, on s'est empressé de nous envoyer ce qu'on appelle des conseillers techniques. Trente ans plus tard nous constatons que c'est l'échec total. Et ces conseillers, c'étaient des experts en matière de politique africaine. Souvent ce sont des anciens administrateurs de l'époque coloniale, ou fils d'administrateurs de l'époque coloniale, ou peut-être qu'ils sont sortis des Grandes Ecoles, de la Sorbonne, ou de Londres, ou des Etats-Unis, ayant fait de l'anthropologie africaine. Quelle peut être l'influence positive d'un tel expert qui est extérieur à ma culture, à mon univers mental, et qui veut conseiller mon gouvernement sur ce qui est bon ou mauvais pour moi, quand il ne sait rien de moi? Ce qui fait donc que cette charge de la race, de la culture, comme on a dit, existe encore.

[I only want to add a small detail. It may be that in my mind I have a conception of whites that is different from the conception in the minds of my American brothers and sisters who live in ghettos. Perhaps they feel more stifled by the Europeans. Since I have my own culture and language, I can withdraw into a world of my own, into what I call the values that offer me refuge. So when I speak up in protest, I can say: "The European is a stranger in my land." But the situation is different in what I know of Afro-American literature from Du Bois up to the present, up to Toni Cade Bambara. In any case, we are merely formulating a very difficult problem.

Today, in 1990, Africa has its flags, national hymns, and governments. This is the time of neocolonialism. I have my own black government, even if it is bad, capitalist, and bourgeois, as well as manipulated by the forces of neocolonialism. After independence everyone eagerly sent us what are known as technical advisers. Thirty years later it is clear to us that this has been a total failure. These advisers were experts in the field of African politics. Often they were former colonial administrators or the sons of those who were administrators in colonial times, or they had degrees from top professional schools, from the Sorbonne, from London or the United States, and had studied African anthropology. What positive influence could such an expert have, since he was an outsider to my culture and my mental universe? And yet he wanted to advise my government on what was good or bad for me, without knowing anything about me. Consequently the burden of race and culture, as Ngugi called it, still persists.]

Question from the Audience: In the film "Mandabi, there is a scene where Dieng goes to the post office to have a letter translated, and Sembène plays the role of the translator. He's seated at a table on which there is a very prominent photo of Che Guevara, the Cuban revolutionary and patriot. The image of Che Guevara in a Dakar post office provokes me to ask, how local or specific an audience does an artist address? For whom is the artistry intended? Would the rural masses in Senegal or in Africa in general recognize that photograph?

Ousmane Sembène: *L'histoire de Che Guevara appartient à l'humanité. Che Guevara est venu à Conakry, en Guinée, c'était au temps de Sékou Touré. Ensuite nous sommes allés à Labé. Je vais vous raconter une anecdote. C'est bien de vivre longtemps. On peut aimer ou ne pas aimer Sékou Touré. Nous avons parcouru le même itinéraire et c'était un ami. Je me trouvais à Conakry. Il y avait la rencontre en Guinée de Sékou Touré, Modibo Keïta, Senghor et l'ancien président de la Mauritanie, Moktar Ould Daddah. Comme je n'habitais pas loin de Sékou Touré il m'a dit: "On va faire une farce à ton ami." Parce que Senghor, il l'appelait mon ami. Et nous voilà partis à Labé très loin, et tous les chefs d'état étaient là. Sékou Touré, qui était sans gêne, me prend par la main et dit: "On va présenter les gens." Che Guevara était derrière moi et il est présenté à Modibo Keïta d'abord, puis à Ould Daddah, et à Senghor, qui a eu le hoquet.*

Si les masses paysannes ne connaissent pas Che Guevara, les citadins des villes
de toute l'Afrique le connaissent, et sa photo, c'est pour mieux le faire connaître! Si
vous entrez chez moi depuis cette époque, j'ai une photo, grande—un mètre carré—
de Che Guevara dans mon salon.

[The story of Che Guevara belongs to all of humanity. Che Guevara came to
Conakry in Guinea during the time of Sékou Touré, and then we went to Labé. I am
going to tell you an anecdote. It's a good thing to live a long life. It is possible to like
or dislike Sékou Touré, but we took the same path in life and he was a friend. I was
in Conakry, and in Guinea a conference was being held with Sékou Touré, Modibo
Keïta, Senghor and the former President of Mauritania, Moktar Ould Daddah. Since
I did not live very far from Sékou Touré, he said: "We're going to play a trick on your
friend." Because he referred to Senghor as my friend. And so we went to Labé, which
was very far, and all the heads of state were there. Sékou Touré, who did not stand on
ceremony, took me by the hand and said: "Let's introduce people to each other." Che
Guevara was behind me and he introduced him first to Modibo Keïta, then to Ould
Daddah, and finally to Senghor, which gave Senghor quite a start.

Even if the rural masses do not know Che Guevara, he is known to the urban
population throughout Africa, and his photograph is in the film to make him even
better known. Since that time, if you come into my house, you will see that I have a
large photograph, one meter square, of Che Guevara in my living room.]

Question from the Audience: Mr. Sembène, many critics have pointed out the
enduring presence of the griot in your works; some even go so far as to call you a
modern griot. To what extent do you consider the griot a model for the modern African
writer, and how can the tradition of the griot be transposed into our technological age?

Ousmane Sembène: *Il faut savoir que toutes les ethnies africaines n'ont pas de griots.*
Je veux bien répondre mais j'aimerais bien poser une question pour mon instruction;
est-ce que dans la société gikuyu il y a des griots? Est-ce que mon ami Ngugi peut nous
informer? Je reviendrai à la réponse.

[We must realize that not all African ethnic groups have griots. I am quite willing
to answer, but for my own education I would like to know if in Gikuyu communities
there is a griot? Can my friend Ngugi enlighten us? I shall come back later to my
answer.]

Ngugi wa Thiong'o: The tradition of the griot is not there in all communities. I suspect
that it is part of those societies in Africa which had a more or less centralized state.
What we have among the Gikuyu is another kind of poetic tradition, which fosters
competition among various poets. Instead of having wrestling matches, you'd have—
as it were—poetic wrestling matches between various regions. In fact, this art was so

highly respected and it was taken so seriously that it was only practiced among that group who had really developed the art of writing. They kept it as part of the guild so that it never spread to the community as a whole.

Ousmane Sembène: *Je pense donc que nous apprenons que sur le continent il y a des groupes qui n'ont pas de griots, dans le sens général du mot. J'ai, du côté de ma mère, les Diola qui n'ont pas de griots, mais ils ont des forgerons. Et du côté de Samba Gadjigo, de sa culture, des Peul, le forgeron est un être inférieur. Donc, vous voyez la différence qui peut exister lorsque vous utilisez une expression en disant qu'elle a une valeur tout à fait continentale. Dans la société wolof il y a des griots. Il y a énormément de couches qui ont le pouvoir de la parole selon les circonstances et les moments. Il y a ceux dont Ngugi vient de parler, qui ont aussi le pouvoir de la joute oratoire, et il y a chez les Wolof un lutteur, un champion lutteur. Il doit être poète. Avant d'affronter son adversaire, il doit lui-même créer ses chansons. Chez les Malinké et les Bambara il y a les* diali, *les forgerons, et il y a aussi les tisserands.*

Ce qui faisait donc que ces griots connaissaient la technique de l'époque. Le travail du fer, du métal ne nous a pas été apporté par l'esclavage ni par la conquête coloniale. Et lorsque parfois les griots se mettaient à parler de la guerre, avant de parler de la bravoure des hommes et des femmes, ils parlaient d'abord de leur armement et du type d'armement et de celui qui avait fabriqué l'armement, et du féticheur ou marabout qui avait béni ces armes. Le griot parlait aussi de l'accoutrement du combattant: quel est le tisserand qui l'a tissé, et quelle est la femme qui a cardé le coton, si c'est la mère, si c'est la femme, si c'est la bien-aimée ou la fiancée. C'est donc vous dire que les griots, en ce moment-là, connaissaient, d'une manière sommaire ou complète, la technique de l'époque. Et si le combat se passait à cheval, ils devaient parler de l'harnachement du cheval. Alors, pour vous parler seulement du rôle du griot, tous ces détails sont très importants dans sa description. A croire que parfois même le griot assistait à l'agonie de son héros.

Laissez-moi vous raconter une légende: Un noble va en guerre, on lui transperce un oeil avec une flèche. Le noble se retourne vers le griot et lui dit: "Regarde, je n'ai pas fermé l'autre," et le griot répond: "Je suis là." On lui crève l'autre oeil, il ne voit plus. Il dit au griot: "Indique-moi quelle direction et je le transperce." Est-ce là une invention imaginaire du griot ou est-ce un témoignage exact? Quoi qu'il en soit, ceci souligne son importance.

Ce que je souhaiterais que les artistes africains empruntent au griot, ce sont ses connaissances, c'est de parler de la femme, de son être intérieur et de son être physique. Que m'importe si Penda est une prostituée, c'est ce qu'elle fait dans la société qui m'intéresse. Dans "Niiwam," la femme, après avoir terrassé son mari, l'enjambe, et ce sont les femmes qui lui disent: "Mais on ne fait pas ça à un homme." Et la femme se retourne: "Mais où est l'homme?"

La jeune fille a un rapport avec son garçon le jour de l'anniversaire de la naissance de Mohammed. On me dit qu'il ne faut pas écrire cela, même si cela a eu lieu. Mais c'est la première nuit qui est la plus intéressante pour les amoureux. Sans blasphémer, pour la mère de Mohammed aussi c'est la nuit la plus intéressante, la naissance de son fils.

Quand je parle des ouvriers, c'est la même chose. Prenez par exemple le cas de ce vieil homme dans Les bouts de bois de Dieu. *Il a travaillé pendant trente années sur le chemin-de-fer et il est mort, mangé par les rats. Mourir mangé par les rats c'est inimaginable parce que le corps d'un mort est sacré. Ce n'est pas sa mort qui m'a été reprochée, c'est le fait que les rats l'aient mangé. Cependant, comme il meurt seul, sans personne pour l'enterrer, il n'y a que les rats, il faut que les rats le mangent. Ici donc, l'opposition entre la machine, l'homme et les rats sert à montrer la nouvelle société.*

De même, quand Abdou Kader Bèye, dans "Xala," fait pousser sa Mercédès ou quand il prend de l'eau d'Evian pour la mettre dans le radiateur de sa voiture, cela fait rire la salle. Là peut-être que je me suis trompé, parce qu'une voiture Mercédès coûte trop cher. Et cette bourgeoisie compradore, ces commis voyageurs du néocolonialisme, trouvent que l'eau qu'ils boivent est trop calcaire pour le radiateur. C'est pourquoi ils utilisent l'Evian. Ils préfèrent soigner cette apparence de richesse, de mimétisme de l'Occident. Donc ce que nous cherchons, ce que je cherche, c'est ce passage maintenant du griot traditionnel, classique, à mon époque.

Nous ne serons plus comme l'Afrique d'avant, l'Afrique ne reviendra jamais en arrière. Nous allons vers l'avant comme tous les peuples. Nous n'avons pas à rattraper l'Occident, nous avons à nous développer nous-mêmes petit à petit. Mais mon travail se situe dans un milieu très difficile.

Pour ce qui est de mon travail, quand j'ai besoin d'en savoir, je vais consulter des experts. Je leur demande et ils m'aident beaucoup. Il en est de même pour la religion musulmane, pour la religion catholique, et pour le droit. J'ai besoin d'avoir une connaissance qui puisse au moins introduire les spectateurs ou le lecteur dans les règles de ce système. La transposition, ce n'est pas moi qui l'amène, c'est le peuple qui l'amène. En dehors de la bataille pour une langue ou des langues africaines tout le reste me vient de mon peuple. Je n'invente rien, et les trois livres sur lesquels je travaille en ce moment et qui doivent sortir ne sont vraiment pas du tout des inventions. C'est tout.

[I think we can learn from this that there are ethnic groups on the continent that do not have griots, in the true sense of the word. Those on my mother's side, that is the Diola, have no griots, but they have blacksmiths. In the case of the Peul, to whom Samba Gadjigo belongs, the blacksmith is an inferior person. So you can see the wide diversity that exists when you want to apply a concept throughout a whole continent.

Within Wolof society we have griots. There are very many different social groups that have the power of the spoken word, depending on different moments and different circumstances. There are those, to whom Ngugi just referred, who also have the power to engage in oratorical contests, and the Wolof have champion wrestlers, who must be poets. Before fighting his adversary such a wrestler has to compose his own songs. The Mandingo, the Bambara have *diali* who are blacksmiths and they also have weavers.

This means that the griots knew the technology of their time. The working of iron and of other metals was not brought to Africa by slavery nor by colonial conquest. At times when the griots spoke of war, before mentioning the bravery of men and women, they would talk about their weapons, the type of weapons they used, identify who had produced those weapons, and also name the diviner or marabout who had blessed them. The griot also talked about the clothing of the combatant, mentioning the weaver who produced the material, and the woman who carded the cotton, whether it was the mother, or the wife, or the sweetheart, or the fiancée. This is to say that the griots of the past were familiar, in general or in detail, with the technology of their time. If the battle was fought on horseback they were expected to describe the way the horse was harnessed. All these details are very important when we describe the function of the griot, to such an extent that at times the griot was present at the death-throes of the hero.

Let me tell you a legend: A nobleman goes to war; one of his eyes is pierced by an arrow. He turns back to the griot and says: "Look at me, I did not close the other eye," and the griot replies: "I am here." His other eye is destroyed and he cannot see any longer. He says to the griot: "Tell me the right direction and I shall pierce the enemy." Is that the griot's invention or is it a true story? In any case, this bears witness to the importance of the griot.

It is this type of knowledge that I would like the African artists to take over from the griot. They should speak about women, about their inner self and their physical self. It does not matter to me whether Penda is a prostitute or not, it is what she does for society that interests me. In "Niiwam," the wife throws her husband down on the floor and then steps over him, and the other women say to her: "You don't do that to a man." She turns around and asks: "Where is there a man here?"

The girl has intercourse with her fiancé on the anniversary of Mohammed's birth. People tell me not to write that even if it happened. But the first night is the most interesting night for lovers, and it is no blasphemy to say that for Mohammed's mother as well it was the best night—the night that led to her son's birth.

It is the same thing when I speak about the workers. The old man in *God's Bits of Wood*, for example, who worked for thirty years on the railroad and who dies, eaten by rats: There is nothing more unthinkable than being eaten by rats because the body of a dead person is sacred. I was blamed not for his death but for having him eaten by rats. He died alone, there was nobody there to bury him, only the rats, so they had to eat him. The machine, human beings, and rats had to be placed in contrast, in order to profile the new society.

When Abdou Kader Bèye, in "Xala," gets people to push his Mercedes, or when he takes Evian water and puts it in the radiator, that makes the audience laugh. But perhaps there I made a mistake because a Mercedes Benz is too expensive. And this comprador *bourgeoisie*, those traveling salesmen of neo-colonialism, believe the water they drink is too hard for the radiator. That is why they use Evian. They would rather keep up this appearance of wealth, this aping of the Western lifestyle. So, what we are looking for, what I am looking for, is a transition from the classical griot to my era.

We will not be like Africa of years past. Africa will not go back. We are moving forward like any other people. It's not a question of catching up with the West. We have to take care of our development by ourselves, step by step. But I carry on my work under very difficult conditions.

When I need information for my work I consult experts and they help me a lot. Whether it is a question of Muslim religious practice, or of Catholicism, or legal matters, I need to get a certain basic knowledge which allows me to introduce my readers or my audience to the way these systems work. The transposition you mentioned will not be effected by me but by the people. Beyond the battle for an African language or for African languages all the rest comes to me from my people. I don't invent anything. The three books I am working on and which will be coming out soon are not inventions. That is all I have to say.]

Samba Gadjigo: During our last night's session Ousmane Sembène did raise an issue which is related to the teaching of African literature in the American universities. Since we are running short of time, I would like to remind our artists if they still wish to discuss or to give their opinion about the issue, now is the time to do so. Who would like to start? . . . We'll start with Ngugi.

Ngugi wa Thiong'o: I can't really talk extensively about the study of African literature in the United States or in the Western world because I have not really been in the teaching profession in this part of the world for long. But my impression is that the teaching of African literature is not really very rooted in the institutions here, although it is probably catching up slowly. The study of that literature is for instance not yet given enough financial backing in terms of staff who are appointed specifically for that literature or department that deals specifically with that literature. So I have the impression that the teaching of African literature is still very much on the margins of the study of literature in the West generally. That's why in my introduction I was saying that it is a pity because what people are really missing is a literature which is, in so many ways, very central to the liberating consciousness of the twentieth century. In fact, in most cases you'll find African literature taught in history departments, in anthropology departments, in archaeology departments, sometimes even in the biological sciences—which is of course a positive comment on African literature if it can fit into all those other departments, but still as a literature it has its own particularities and therefore it needs to be seen as part of literature generally. It's not just African literature; I get the impression that it is the literature of black people as a whole which is still marginalized and has not been given the resources necessary to make it be part of the central institutions of the West. As I have said, the sensibility which this literature represents is actually the sensibility of the majority even in the West in so far as it's the sensibility of struggle, and such a struggle is part of the majority in the West and in the world generally.

Where African literature is taught, the question of interpretation arises, and of course this depends very much on people's individual ideologies—ideological positions on the various issues in the world. This does, of course, affect how this literature is interpreted when it's actually taught. As far as the knowledge of African languages is concerned, I'm always amazed—in a way this is a comment on the special predicament of the African situation—that it's only when it comes to expertise in African literature, African history, African anthropology, or whatever that experts, both Western and unfortunately also African, do not have to know African languages at all. In almost any other area of expertise in the world it would be inconceivable for someone to say that he or she was an expert in Chinese history without a knowledge of Chinese. In the case of French, I can't conceive of someone saying, "I'm really the leading authority on French culture and literature," and has no knowledge of French at all. Yet, in the case of Africa, it's the exact opposite: people will plead ignorance. Maybe it's part of the predicament of the Third World really that the world is dominated by a handful of European or Western nations, and in the realm of culture, a handful of European languages dominate the world. I was talking the other day at Penn State University to the annual meeting of the Comparative Literature Association. And I was pointing out in my talk that these departments tend to be dominated by German, French, and English: those languages which again historically are associated with colonization and the domination of the world. Comparative literature departments, to be genuinely comparative, need to open out to literatures of post-colonial societies, and even more so to the languages of post-colonial societies.

Ousmane Sembène: *Venons-en à la question sur l'enseignement de la littérature africaine dans les universités américaines: Après plusieurs observations, je constate que ceux que nous appelons les Africanistes ne connaissent rien de l'Afrique. Le long de l'année je les vois parcourir le Sénégal et venir poser des questions. Comme l'a dit mon ami Ngugi, on ne peut pas enseigner une culture si on n'en possède pas la langue.*

Il faut mettre les littératures africaines sur le même pied d'égalité que les autres littératures du monde et ne pas les considérer comme des littératures marginales. C'est peut-être bien de m'inviter mais je connais des professeurs africains qui connaissent mieux que moi la littérature africaine parce que c'est leur spécialité. La base de la littérature, c'est la civilisation et la culture. La culture, c'est la langue. Ces professeurs africanistes, malgré leur meilleure volonté, me rappellent un peu les ethnographes qui, au début du siècle, parcouraient l'Afrique et, sans aucune analyse, montraient mes parents, mon père, ma grand-mère et tout ça en train de danser avec des feuilles de banane là où je pense, et qui disaient que les Africains passent leur temps à danser, oubliant que ce sont eux qui ont détruit des capitales, des constructions et des cultures.

Quand je suis entré par ici, je crois avoir lu que cette partie de l'Université a été fondée en 1827. Je ne sais pas si c'est vrai ou non, ou si j'ai mal lu. Chaka est mort en 1827. Samouri est né en 1830. Je peux vous donner des dates où des hommes ont lutté pour notre indépendance, et quand je demande cette question aux professeurs qui enseignent des cultures africaines, ils disent: "I don't know."

Peut-être qu'on peut nous enseigner la technique ici, et c'est vrai, parce que mon fils a appris la technique aux Etats-Unis pendant quatre années, et il a fait six ans en Union Soviétique. Je pense que c'est un enfant techniquement riche et ce n'est plus moi, parce que moi j'ai vu mon père se décoiffer devant le blanc, tandis que moi, j'ai refusé de me décoiffer devant le blanc. Je pense que mon fils ne tombera même pas sa veste devant le blanc.

Et à ces africanistes, je leur demanderais d'étudier, de connaître les langues africaines et de ne plus faire l'amalgame, parce que les ethnologues d'il y a cent ans ont menti et aux blancs et aux noirs. Ils ont été les pourvoyeurs d'un complexe de supériorité et d'un complexe d'infériorité. Ils ont dit aux blancs: voilà votre civilisation, elle est supérieure à celle des noirs, et aux noirs: votre culture est inférieure à celle des blancs.

Maintenant quand je regarde sur les plages de Dakar ou de l'Afrique, je vois que nos femmes sont habillées et que ce sont les blanches qui sont nues. Donc, je peux faire de l'ethnographie pour dire à mes femmes: vous êtes mieux habillées et tout ce qui va avec cela. Elles sont nues parce qu'elles ont besoin de beaucoup de soleil, moi j'en ai trop, c'est tout. Cela fait donc partie de ma création. Mais je leur demanderais, mon dieu, d'étudier les cultures et les langues africaines et de ne plus vous induire en erreur. Je leur demanderai aussi d'étudier les Afro-Américains, de les connaître mieux, de savoir ce qu'ils pensent, ce qu'ils écrivent.

On nous a canalisés vers la danse, la musique. Dès qu'il y a une musique quelque part, s'il y a un noir, on se retourne pour voir s'il bouge les fesses. Ils nous ont tellement influencés que même dans les accoutrements vous voyez déjà l'habillement de l'Africain plus ou moins complexé. Je souhaiterais une culture qui ne nous laisse pas en paix, ni blancs, ni noirs.

Car qu'est-ce que c'est que la culture? C'est ce dont nous avons besoin du jour de notre naissance à notre mort. Dans les quatre langues africaines que je parle, il n'y pas de mot qui signifie culture. La culture, c'est une succession de situations. Donnons des exemples: La manière d'être à table, pour vous, c'est pour moi la manière d'être sur une natte. La seule façon dont l'épouse pose le plat suffit à vous donner de l'appétit ou à vous le couper. Tenez, vous rentrez chez vous, votre femme vous dit sans cérémonie: voilà à manger. Déjà cela vous coupe l'appétit. Ou le mari qui vient avec ses fleurs (parce que vous avez le langage des fleurs), arrive devant sa femme et laisse tomber le bouquet de fleurs, en disant: c'est pour toi. Et c'est là le langage gestuel qui n'a pas besoin d'être parlé, mais qui se comprend. Chez nous, nous aimons bien nous habiller, mais ce n'est pas pour moi, c'est pour l'autre. Voilà donc une autre expression de ma culture. Ma façon de saluer l'homme ou la femme, ma façon de me comporter avec quelqu'un qui est plus jeune que moi ou plus âgé que moi. Et cela dans toutes les langues. Les mots sont chargés d'un potentiel de violence, et de douceur poétique aussi. Cela dépend de la façon de les employer. Dans toutes les langues, on peut dire je t'aime, mais on ne peut pas dire je t'aime en faisant des gestes agressifs. Je pense donc que ceux qui enseignent la littérature africaine, ou les civilisations africaines, doivent faire un effort pour comprendre tout ceci.

Je demanderai aux universitaires de faire une thèse sur le sujet suivant: Comment les blancs perçoivent et enseignent la culture africaine quand ils n'en parlent pas les langues? Et je leur demanderai aussi de connaître la culture noire américaine. Voilà une culture qui a donné à ce siècle la plus belle chose qui puisse exister au monde et qu'aucune autre culture n'a donné, c'est le jazz. Il est né du monde culturel noir américain. Pendant des années personne n'en voulait, c'était le chant ou les Blues dans les champs de coton. Maintenant vous avez le jazz chinois, le jazz japonais, même chez la reine d'Angleterre on joue le jazz. A l'Elysée on joue le jazz, à la Maison Blanche on joue le jazz. Voilà une relation de culture à civilisation.

Beaucoup de musiciens européens, quand ils ont voulu comprendre le jazz, sont venus s'établir aux Etats-Unis, avec les noirs. Ils ont appris la langue, ils ont appris la musique, ils ont appris l'intonation de la voix. C'est l'héritage du monde. Donc voilà ce que notre monde à venir nous incite à faire. Je pense que maintenant nous voyons la grande cantatrice Jessye Norman qui a chanté la Marseillaise - j'étais à Paris avec elle. Il y a deux mille ans, où étaient les parents de cette femme? Mais maintenant la voilà, tout le monde la reçoit. Aussi est-ce un gain pour l'humanité. Voilà donc tout ce que nous avons à faire. La culture ne sert qu'à cela, d'être bien ensemble.

[As far as the teaching of African literature in American universities is concerned: From what I have observed, those we call Africanists know nothing of Africa. All year long we see them traveling through Senegal, asking questions. As my friend Ngugi has said, you cannot teach a culture if you do not master the language. African literatures must be treated like other world literatures and not considered marginal literatures. It may be a good thing to invite me, but I know African professors who know African literature better than I do, because that is their profession. Culture and civilization are the foundation of literature. Culture is language, and these Africanist professors, despite their best intentions, remind me a little of those ethnographers who, at the beginning of the century, used to travel around Africa and depicted my relatives, my father, my grandmother, and many others dancing with banana leaves stuck you know where. They did not analyze what they saw and they said that Africans spend all their time dancing. They were oblivious of the fact that it was they who destroyed capital cities, buildings, and entire cultures.

When I came here I think I read—I don't remember where—that this part of the University was founded in 1827. I don't know if this is true or not, or if I misread. Chaka died in 1827. Samori was born in 1830. I can give you dates on which men fought for our independence, but when I ask these professors who are teaching African culture, they say: "I don't know."

Perhaps we can be taught technology here. That is so, as a matter of fact, since my son learned technology in the United States for four years and also studied for six years in the Soviet Union. I think he is technologically well endowed. He is not in my situation because I saw my father take his hat off to white people, while I have refused to do so. I think that my son will not even take his jacket off when he meets a white man.

As for those Africanists, I would tell them to study and master African languages and no longer throw all of Africa into the same pot, because the ethnologists of the last century lied both to the blacks and to the whites. They were the purveyors of both a superiority and an inferiority complex. They told the white people: "Your civilization is superior to that of the blacks," and to the black people they said: "Your culture is inferior to that of the whites."

When I now observe the beaches in Dakar or in Africa generally, I see that our women are dressed while white women are naked. Now I too could engage in ethnography and tell our women: "You are better dressed, and all that goes with it." But all it really means is that white women are undressed because they need a lot of sun, while I have too much sun. So this is a part of the way I was created. I would ask Africanists to really study African languages and cultures, and not to lead you astray any longer. They should also study Afro-Americans, to know them better, to know what they are thinking, what they are writing.

We have been channeled towards music and dance. Whenever there is music somewhere, if there is someone around who is black, people turn to look whether he is wiggling his buttocks. We have been so strongly influenced that it has given Africans a complex even in the way they dress. I wish for a culture that does not leave any of us at ease, whether we are black or white.

What is culture? It is what we need from the day of our birth to the day of our death. In the four African languages I speak there is no word for culture, because culture consists of a succession of situations. Take the way people sit down to a meal, which for me means sitting on a mat. The way in which the wife puts down the dish is enough to make you either lose or get an appetite. You come home and your wife just says: "Here is your food." That already makes you lose your appetite. And in your case, since you use the language of flowers, the husband who comes home, just drops the flowers in front of his wife and says: "This is for you." These are examples of a language of gestures that do not require speech but are understood. Back home we like to be well dressed, but we do not do it for ourselves, we do it for other people. That is another expression of my culture, as is the way I greet a woman or a man, the way I behave with someone who is younger or older than I. This is true in all languages. Words are loaded with a potential for violence, and also for poetic gentleness. It depends on how we use them. In all languages we can say, "I love you," but not with aggressive gestures. So I believe that those who teach African literature or African civilization have to make an effort to understand all this.

I would ask academics to write a thesis on the following question: How do whites perceive and teach African culture when they do not speak African languages? I would also ask them to know African-American culture. That is a culture that has made the most beautiful contribution in the world to this century, one which has been made by no other culture. I am talking about jazz, which originated in the cultural world of black America. For years no one was interested. Jazz was merely a kind of song and Blues in the cotton fields. Now there is Chinese jazz, Japanese jazz, and jazz is played even at the court of the Queen of England, at the Elysée Palace, and at the White House. This is how culture relates to civilization.

When they wanted to understand jazz, many European musicians came to the United States to be among black people. They learned both the language and the music, and they learned the right intonation. It is a heritage shared by all of humanity. This is what we are called upon to do for the world of the future. Recently we saw the great singer Jessye Norman sing the Marseillaise—I was with her in Paris. Where were the forebears of this woman two thousand years ago? Now here she is being welcomed by everyone, and that is a gain for all mankind. This is all we have to do. To get along together in harmony is the sole purpose of culture.]

Toni Cade Bambara: I think that while we're at it we might also talk about film—the teaching of African film or Third World film in the film schools around the country. It's curious that at this point in time, if you were abroad most anywhere and took a degree in American studies, the literature you would be reading for American literature would be black literature. And that's true at the University of Tokyo, University of Havana—you bet, University of Peking, Catholic University in Rio de Janeiro, a whole lot of universities. It is assumed that you cannot be conversant in American studies, not be grounded in American reality, without a thoroughgoing knowledge of African-American literature. That of course is not true here.

This parallels or echoes the same situation with music: that in most parts of the world there was a recognition of black improvisational music or what some people call jazz as the great art form of this country, certainly the authentic music of this place. It was a good thirty-two years or one and a half generations before this country caught up with that knowledge, but then began to use black improvisational music to make propaganda more palatable, that is to say the USIA began to send jazz combos around the world, began to use music as part of its "Voice of America" barrage, and of course what with the Motown sound Corporate pop, we know now why Coca Cola would like to teach the world to sing in perfect harmony.

This next wave has been the film. The filmmakers in my neighborhood are better known in Peking than they are in my neighborhood, and that's an aspect of USA-style apartheid. They're better known in Paris, in Holland, in Britain, in Canada than they are in the major film schools in this country, even those filmmakers who have caused a great deal of articles to be written in fairly prestigious journals, who have stopped the show at Cannes Film Festivals, who have garnered all kinds of medals at the Berlin Film Festival *et cetera*, are still not taught here. So as you say, Ngugi, it's not just the African languages, it's not just the particular situation of African people, it is the nature of that same war.

Earl Lovelace: I think Ngugi was saying a while ago that it appeared to be absurd that a handful of European languages should dominate Africa. Well, I think that is as absurd as the fact that a handful of European nations continue dominating Africa and the world. I think that what we're talking about really is the continuing of a colonial relationship, which seems to suggest to people who have been in power that they can understand those over whom they have exercised power, that they are simple people, and that those who used to be in power can say and do what they want. And I don't know to whom we are complaining, that is the other question. I don't know if we want to ask people who have been teaching or interpreting Africa and whom we view as European to go and get a better course—to learn your lessons better, you know, learn your languages more carefully—and then come back and present a view of Africa. I think that if that has to be done, it has to be done firstly by an engagement of African people themselves: to enter the world and to give it a view of the world, a view that contends with the existing view, and it seems to me that that is what is going to change the world. I don't know how well we are capable or fitted to do this because I've been hearing from here, for example, terms like slavery, roots of slavery, the slave master, and things like that. Now who is this master? The notion of master which I have heard people talk about is in terms of black people and white people, and it is assumed that one will say, "Okay, this white slave master." For me the term master connotes mastery over something; it suggests that one is following him, that he is to be followed, and it seems to me that the experience of Africans in relation to Europeans and the relationship of their struggle against enslavement has exactly not been to follow him, but to have themselves a different view of where they should go. I don't know how we continue with this language and expect to change anything.

John Wideman: All I'll say is, "Amen." The intellectual bankruptcy of the University is well documented, if any one cares to examine this on most issues important to us—sex, race, gender—we'll find that intellectual bankruptcy is not an accident, it's a tradition and, in fact, what else would we expect, given the fact that universities have this sort of top-down notion of expertise and control. The people who go through them are "clients," what is taught there are not necessities, but something to get you through a certain kind of very predictable bourgeois existence, and they're not the places where change, social change, has ever come from except when that change has been one way or another forced out into the street, into the people's hearts. I was in South Africa recently and I got this sense of change as opposed to what we are looking for in the University. Mandela said that he had been using the phrase "power to the people" for many years and thought he understood it, but only within the last few months as he sat in a prison cell did he realize that he was going to be liberated from that cell not by Mr. De Klerk's generosity but by the power of the people and that he could sit in that cell every day and feel that power getting stronger and stronger. Then he began to know really what power of the people meant. Why are we looking to the University for the power of change, for the power to change things?

Toni Cade Bambara: I wanted to respond to what John said. Why do we expect change in a university? Because the war has to be fought on every front. One of the difficulties we face, whoever we are—organizers, mobilizers, creators of thought, contenders, warriors with an oppositional culture—one of the things that we're struggling to come to grips with these days is from whence will come the kind of analysis that really tells us accurately where we are at this point in time in this country. We're at that stage where we really need a very holistic view of the various spheres of contestation and battle in this country. Nobody quite has it, but we do know, for example, that when a great deal of agitation takes place, for example in the legislative arena, that we might gain there, but it won't get picked up, or it won't be reflected in personal relationships. Or where the feminist movement gains ground and maybe even consolidates some ground with that struggle around gender issues, if the question of racism—white supremacy, let's get real!—is not also fearlessly addressed in that battle, that affliction, that pathology can begin to... you know what I'm saying, back that up! So we're in a process, we're in a moment now, it seems to me, where there needs to be a constant attention to the whole structure and where there need to be tremendous kinds of dialogues going on in terms of coalitions which have never been forged before. This is it. The University may not continue in this bogus way recruiting people to be trained in the delusional systems, to bolster a totally fraudulent version of reality, of human beings, of what human nature is; the war is fought here too. There is no margin, *there is no margin*; there's no safe place to be anywhere and that is one of the reasons I feel kind of sorry for people caught up in the universities who think they're safe. I'm thinking particularly of all these Africanists who think that their days have long since been numbered, everything's over but the bleeding. At these conferences you see people still swaggering about attempting to silence people from the margin, as they say. The margin's at the center—it's a new day.

Ngugi wa Thiong'o: I'll just add on to that very quickly and say that while I agree absolutely that, of course, the battlefield finally is really in the streets, let's remember—since we are talking about the dialectics of form and content—what happens at the universities can also, in fact, influence what is going on in the streets and vice versa. Let me just take a very simple case: We may think there is no connection between the peasant in Africa and universities like where we are today. But take a student from Africa who gets his parents to sell their cows to get him to higher education in Africa and then on to America. And he or she enters a literature department here and finds that those who are in the literary canon, or who represent the great tradition, completely exclude the literature of African Americans. So he or she goes away thinking that the only African-American writer who belongs to the canon of the mainstream is Ralph Ellison. For a long time *Invisible Man* was the only novel which used to be represented as part of their literature. The same student who has come here to gather knowledge takes that knowledge back to a remote village or center of culture in Africa and he goes to teach literature. What will he be teaching? He too will exclude what is genuinely his heritage from what he will be imparting to African students in the centers of culture or wherever they come from. This is a narrow example, but we can actually see that what happens at universities is very, very crucial; in fact, universities are ideological factories where very important ideological battles have been fought, are still being fought, and will be fought.

John Wideman: I want to perhaps clarify and dialogue. Number one, I was trying to address. . .well, number one, if universities were burned to the ground today I wouldn't get a check next Friday—so already I'm ambivalent about losing the university. But what I was attempting to address is the sense of surprise and outrage and the kind of frustration that universities aren't at the leading edge, that they aren't other than they are. That shouldn't be a surprise anymore and that's what I was attempting to address. My son is going to a very good and expensive school in America—Brown University—he is doing Afro-American studies. He decided that there wasn't enough there; he wanted to go back to the source. He learned enough there to want to go back to the source and so he attempted to do a year abroad in Africa, and he thought a program was set up, but at the last minute it collapsed, so he wound up going to SOAS in London—the School of Oriental and African Studies. He was hoping there to get back to the roots, but in fact he found out there's a systematic racist policy at SOAS. And he's been instrumental in uncovering that sham, the documents on record, and showing that African voices are not allowed to be part of that education. And I think that's something very important and I support him in that and I'm proud of that. But he did not go there in a posture of being surprised and disappointed that SOAS didn't offer him what he wanted. When he found something that he didn't like, he knew what the next step was.

Question from the Audience: Mr. Sembène, beyond your role as a writer and filmmaker, what sort of influence can you and other African artists have on the burning political issues of the day? The war in Eritrea or the one in the Western Sahara come to mind as examples.

Ousmane Sembène: *On va essayer de répondre. En ce qui concerne l'Eritrée il faut voir l'ensemble du continent africain et les textes signés par les chefs d'état africains que Nyerere a appelés "le syndicat des chefs d'état." Est-ce qu'ils reconnaissent les frontières héritées du colonialisme?*

Dans les années à venir trois pôles vont se poser: premièrement l'Eritrée, deuxièmement le Soudan, le sud et le nord, et enfin l'histoire du Polisario: le Maroc, l'Algérie et la Mauritanie. Je ne sais pas ce qui se passe dans les autres états africains. Mais je sais que dans les journaux indépendants du Sénégal nous parlons de l'Eritrée, nous parlons du Soudan, nous parlons du Polisario. Nous n'avons pas de solutions. La solution relève en partie de la politique des états. Mais je sais qu'au Sénégal il y a des jeunes qui soutiennent le combat de l'Eritrée et je sais que dans nos manifestations cinématographiques nous invitons les représentants de l'Eritrée à participer au même pied d'égalité que les autres états. Comme notre ami Med Hondo avait fait un film pour le Polisario, il dépendra des amis de l'Eritrée de nous demander comment faire un film pour eux, pour qu'ils puissent s'exprimer. Nous pouvons aller jusque là, mais pas au-delà. Nous connaissons la nature du drame qui se passe en Eritrée. En tout cas, venant de l'Afrique voilà notre position. Mais nous n'avons pas ignoré l'Eritrée, nous n'ignorons pas le Soudan, nous n'ignorons pas le Polisario. Voilà ma réponse sur cette question.

[I will try to answer. On the question of Eritrea we have to look at the whole of the African continent and at documents signed by the African heads of state—"the trade union of heads of state," as Nyerere called them. Do these documents recognize the legitimacy of the borders inherited from colonialism?

In the coming years three issues are going to be brought to the fore: First of all Eritrea, secondly South and North Sudan, and then the problem of the Polisario: Morocco, Algeria, and Mauritania. I don't know what is going on in other African countries, but I do know that in the independent newspapers of Senegal we write about Eritrea, about the Sudan, and about the Polisario. We have no solutions. The solution depends in part on affairs of state. But I do know that in Senegal there are young people who support the struggle of the Eritrean people, and I know that for our film showings we invite representatives of Eritrea to participate on an equal footing with other states in Africa. Just as our friend Med Hondo made a film for the Polisario, it is up to our friends from Eritrea to ask us how we could produce a film for them so they could express themselves. We can go that far but we cannot go any further. We are aware of the tragic situation. In any case, that is our position as Africans. But we have not ignored Eritrea, we do not ignore the Sudan, nor the Polisario. That is my answer to this question.]

PART THREE

OUSMANE SEMBÈNE'S REMARKS AFTER THE SHOWING OF HIS FILM "CAMP DE THIAROYE"

Ce film que nous venons de voir retrace une histoire vraie. Mais avant de vous en parler je veux mentionner les pays qui ont participé à ce film. Il y a un acteur noir américain, des Américains blancs, et des acteurs français. Et les acteurs noirs africains que vous venez de voir, viennent du Congo, du Gabon, de la Côte d'Ivoire, du Niger, du Burkina Faso, du Bénin, du Mali, de la Guinée et du Sénégal. Ceci était la configuration de ceux qu'on a appelé les "tirailleurs sénégalais" et qui ont participé à la dernière guerre 1939-45. Et comme nous venons de le voir, ils ont été tués. Ces hommes ont été, si vous voulez, les premiers levains du mouvement de la lutte pour l'indépendance. Ils venaient d'être libérés en août, 1944, et puis on les a tués en décembre, 1944, en plein règne du Général de Gaulle. Et pour nous donc, que ce soit de Gaulle, Mitterrand, ou Pétain, c'est la même chose. Cette dualité qui a existé entre les soldats noirs et les officiers blancs découle du système colonial qui a duré à peu près cent ans. Ces officiers blancs avaient l'habitude de frapper les noirs et d'ignorer en eux tout sentiment de dignité.

Mais ces soldats noirs ont été envoyés au front, pour participer à la libération de l'Europe. Pendant leur séjour au front ils ont fréquenté d'autres Européens. Ils ont vu des familles, de lâches ou de braves Européens. Et lorsqu'ils sont retournés chez eux, ils n'étaient plus les mêmes. Ils ne pouvaient plus accepter ce qu'ils avaient accepté avant de partir. Et ils n'avaient plus de respect pour ces officiers qui n'avaient pas participé à la guerre. Voilà tout le malentendu.

C'est-à-dire que dans l'histoire du cinéma, si vous voulez, particulièrement en Europe, vous pouvez voir des films tournés pendant la guerre 1914-18. S'il y a des noirs, ils sont des ombres qui passent. Pendant la dernière guerre, 1939-45, c'était la même chose. Même dans les films américains tournés pendant ces deux guerres, les noirs n'étaient que des ombres. De même, dans les films que n'approuvaient pas les Américains pendant la guerre du Vietnam, les noirs qui participaient étaient toujours là en ombre, pour justifier qu'il y avait des noirs; ce n'étaient pas des personnages. Donc, on peut dire que dans l'histoire du cinéma, le noir n'était qu'un danseur ou une ombre qui passe.

Ce temps est révolu. L'histoire du monde est faite de tout le monde, de toutes les races. Nous allons extraire de l'histoire notre participation, mais ce sera votre histoire, à vous aussi. Nous ne dirons pas comme Langston Hughes: "Les gens mangent à table, et nous, nous allons à la cuisine." Maintenant on va partager la salle à manger et la cuisine. Pour qu'ils comprennent qu'on doit avoir sa part; toutes nos filles et nos garçons—noirs et blancs—dansent à la même musique. Pour l'Afrique, c'est la première fois que nous présentons notre histoire. Et quand je présentais ce film pour la première fois, à Dakar, l'Ambassadeur de France a quitté la salle. Cependant, nous ne le faisions ni par haine ni par esprit de vengeance. Mais c'est pour l'histoire de tous les peuples du monde. C'est un témoignage de notre passé dans l'histoire.

Tenez, j'ai deux histoires, deux anecdotes à vous raconter: Pendant la guerre, à Dakar, il y avait des soldats blancs et noirs américains. Il y a une dizaine d'années, lors de mon dernier passage aux Etats-Unis, un Américain blanc est venu m'approcher, et il m'a dit, "Mais, vous habitez Yoff?" (Yoff, c'est un petit village de pécheurs à côté de l'ancien camp de l'armée américaine). Et ce blanc avait des amis dans ce village. Il allait chez eux. Il m'a bien parlé du village. Nous avons pris le pot ensemble. Je lui ai demandé s'il connaissait le ghetto noir ici, aux Etats-Unis. Il m'a dit, "Non." Je lui ai dit, "Comment? Vous connaissez les noirs qui sont loin, et vous ne pouvez pas connaître vos voisins?" Il m'a dit, "Ce n'est pas pareil." J'ai demandé, "Mais où est la différence?" Il m'a dit, "Je ne peux pas parler avec eux." Ça m'a surpris. J'ai dit, "Vous parlez américain, tous les deux." Il m'a dit, "Tu ne peux pas comprendre." Et je n'ai pas compris non plus! Il m'a donné un message pour la famille qui l'avait hébergé à Yoff, car ils sont restés en correspondance. Ce qui fait que des fois, on préfère aller plus loin pour comprendre les gens que de comprendre nos voisins.

Revenons à notre film: le noir américain qui joue ce rôle, grâce à mes amis américains qui l'ont choisi et envoyé, avec son accord, est venu d'Angleterre par Boeing. En toute liberté. Il a travaillé avec nous et on lui a dit, "Tu es venu par avion, mais tes ancêtres sont partis au fond des cargos d'esclaves." Et puis nous l'avons amené dans la maison des esclaves à Gorée. Et il a pleuré. Quand il a fini de pleurer, on lui a demandé pourquoi il avait pleuré. Il a dit, "Mais, c'est ici, les esclaves sont partis d'ici." Je lui ai dit, "C'est l'avenir qui nous intéresse. Nous, nous avons gardé cette maison seulement comme témoignage, et non pas pour pleurer." Par ailleurs, quand on a projeté ce film en Côte d'Ivoire, un spectateur est sorti et est allé gifler un blanc. On lui a demandé pourquoi il avait fait cela. Parce que, a-t-il dit, il avait mal au cœur. Et on lui a dit, "Va à l'hôpital d'Abidjan. Il y a beaucoup de gens qui meurent de rien." Et moi, quand je vois la basilique construite par un Président noir, moi j'ai envie d'aller à l'hôpital.

On ne fait pas une histoire pour se venger, mais pour s'enraciner. Voilà pourquoi nous avons fait ce film pour le monde entier et non pour une race; c'est pour que vous sachiez que les noirs ont participé à la guerre, et que nous n'avons pas fini avec notre histoire qui est aussi la vôtre. Nous espérons partir au mois de juillet à New York en première mondiale. Et nous voulons inviter tous les anciens combattants, blancs et noirs. Le reste du film vous appartient, il ne m'appartient plus, ni à mon équipe.

J'ajouterai seulement que ces hommes ne mourront plus maintenant, grâce au cinéma. Les Français les ont tués, mais le cimetière existe encore à Dakar. Nous l'entretenons toujours, mais mon gouvernement n'en dit rien. Il n'existe sur aucun papier officiel. On ne vient pas fleurir les tombes. Jusqu'à ce film, c'étaient des tombes anonymes. Maintenant, elles ne sont plus anonymes. Quand nous recevons des amis, nous leur disons, "Allons visiter le cimetière de Thiaroye," et ils vont voir le cimetière. Il y a des tombes et des croix. Il n'y a ni noms, ni matricules. Mais c'est la mémoire de l'histoire. Et cela nous le gardons.

[The film we just saw tells a true story. But before talking to you about the story I want to mention the countries that took part in this. There is an Afro-American actor, there are white American and French actors. The black African actors you just saw come from the Congo, Gabon, the Ivory Coast, Niger, Mali, Guinea, and Senegal. This was the make-up of the troops known as the *tirailleurs sénégalais*, who participated in the last war, 1939-45, and who were killed, as we have just seen in the film. Those men were the first leaven, so to speak, of the independence movement. They had just been released, in August 1944, and they were murdered in December 1944, while de Gaulle was in power. De Gaulle, Mitterrand or Pétain, that makes no difference to us. The duality that existed between the black soldiers and the white officers is a result of the colonial system that lasted almost a century. These white officers were in the habit of beating blacks and ignoring that they had any feelings of dignity.

But those same black soldiers were sent into battle to participate in the liberation of Europe. During their stay in Europe, they mingled with other Europeans. They saw them in their families, they saw cowards and brave Europeans. And when they returned home, they were no longer the same. Now they could not accept what they accepted before they left for Europe. And they no longer felt any respect for these white officers who had not participated in the war. That created the misunderstanding between the two groups.

What I mean is that in the history of the cinema, particularly European cinema, you can see that if there are black people in the films made during the war of 1914-18, they appear as fleeting shadows. The same thing is true of the last war. Even American films made during these two wars feature black people only as shadows. Even in films made during the Vietnam war without American approval, the blacks who appear are still shadows, introduced merely to justify that blacks took part in the war; they are not really central to the movie. So we can say that in the history of cinema, black people were only dancers or fleeting shadows.

That time is over now. The history of the world involves everyone, all races. We are going to highlight our participation in history, but it will also be your history. We are not going to say like Langston Hughes: "People are sitting down at the dinner table, but we go off to the kitchen."[52] Now we are going to share both the dining room *and* the kitchen. And so that people understand that everyone must have a share, all our daughters and sons dance to the same music — whether they are white or black. For us Africans this is the first time that we present our own history. When I showed this film for the first time, in Dakar, the French Ambassador left the theater. Yet we did not put on the film out of hatred or in a spirit of vengeance, but for the sake of the history of all the people in the world. It bears witness to our past in the history of mankind.

I have two anecdotes to tell you. During the war there were white and black American soldiers in Dakar. About ten years ago, during my last visit to the United States, a white American approached me and said, "Don't you live in Yoff?" (Yoff is a small fishing village close to the former American military base.) This white man had friends in the village, and he used to go and visit them, and he seemed to know the village well. We had a drink together. I asked him if he knew the black ghetto here in the United States. He told me "No." And I said, "How can this be? You know black people who live far away, and you don't know your neighbors?" He said, "It's not the same thing." I asked him, "Where is the difference?" He said, "I cannot talk to them." That was a surprise for me. I said, "Both you and they speak American English." He said to me, "You don't understand." And truly I did not understand. He gave me a message for the family that had hosted him in Yoff, because they kept in touch by correspondence. You see that sometimes we prefer to go far away to understand people rather than understanding our neighbors.

To come back to the film: The black American who is playing the role of a black American arrived from England in a Boeing jet, thanks to my American friends who chose him and sent him, with his agreement and of his own free choice. He worked with us and we said to him, "You came by plane, but your ancestors left here in the hulls of slave ships." We took him to the slave house in Gorée. And he wept. When he was through we asked him why he cried. He said, "Because this is the place from which the slaves left." And I told him, "What matters to us is the future. We kept this place only as a memorial to the past, not to cry over it." Incidentally, when this film was shown in the Ivory Coast, one man in the audience went out of the theater, saw a white man, and went and slapped him. And we asked him why he did that. He said he was sick at heart. We told him, "Go to the hospital of Abidjan and you will see that a lot of people are dying for no reason at all." As for me, when I see the cathedral built by a black President[53] I feel sick enough to go off to the hospital myself.

You don't create a story to take revenge but in order to be rooted in your own history and culture. That is why we made this film for the whole world, not for any one race. So that you should know that blacks participated in the war and that we are not done yet with our history, which is your history as well. We hope to put on the world premiere of this film in July, in New York. And we want to invite all the war veterans, white as well as black. Beyond this the film belongs to you and no longer to me or to my crew.

All I wish to add is that these men will no longer be dead, thanks to the cinema. The French killed them, but they still have a cemetery in Dakar. We still take care of it, but my government says nothing about that cemetery and it does not appear on any official document. No one comes to place flowers on their graves. Until this film they were nameless. No longer. Now when we have friends visiting, we say, "Let's go to the cemetery of Thiaroye," and they come with us to look at it. There are graves and crosses, but no names or military identification numbers. But this is the memory of history, which we keep alive.]

PART FOUR

AN INTERVIEW WITH OUSMANE SEMBÈNE BY SADA NIANG
Toronto, July 1992

"De tout temps, le refus a été le signe d'une dignité fondamentale."
["Since the dawn of times, refusal has been a sign of fundamental dignity."]

Sada Niang: *Ousmane Sembène, je voudrais d'abord savoir quelles conditions et quelles raisons vous ont poussé à écrire* Le docker noir?
[Ousmane Sembène, could you tell us what motivated you to write *The Black Docker*?]

Ousmane Sembène: *Je travaillais au port de Marseille; j'étais docker. C'était dur de faire un travail manuel lourd au port de Fos et de vouloir écrire en même temps. Il a fallu donc beaucoup de volonté de ma part pour mener à bout ce travail. Quant aux motivations, le fait était que jusque là, à ma connaissance, toute la littérature africaine écrite était basée sur une Afrique folklorique, bon enfant. Il s'agissait, dans ces oeuvres, d'une Afrique qui attendait tout de l'Europe, qui n'avait aucune conscience de la patrie et de sa personnalité. C'était une Afrique assimilée que l'Europe avait déjà gagnée et corrodée de l'intérieur. Pour moi c'était révoltant, car cette littérature ethnographique présentait les Africains comme des enfants qu'il fallait aider.* Batouala *de René Maran était peut-être le seul livre qui pouvait apporter quelque changement dans cette image de l'Afrique. Mais même ici, le chien avait plus d'importance que Batouala. Tout ceci m'a profondément révolté.*

[I was working at the Marseilles harbor where I was a docker. It was difficult to perform hard manual labor at the Fos harbor and write at the same time. Hence it took strong determination on my part to finish this project. As to what motivated me, the fact was that, to my knowledge, the whole body of written African literature rested on a folkloric and simple-minded image of Africa. Africa in these works was a continent which expected everything from Europe, devoid of any patriotic consciousness, unaware of itself. This Africa had been assimilated, won over and corroded inside out by Europe. This type of ethnographic literature upset me greatly because it turned Africans into children who needed assistance. Perhaps *Batouala* by René Maran was the exception. But even there, the dog is more important than Batouala himself. All of this upset me deeply.]

Sada Niang: *Aviez-vous publié d'autres oeuvres avant* Le docker noir?
[Had you published anything before *The Black Docker*?]

Ousmane Sembène: *Je participais effectivement à un mouvement anti-colonialiste et dans ce cadre, j'avais publié des poèmes dans le premier numéro de* Peuples opprimés. *C'était une revue liée à l'époque aux* Cahiers du Sud, *à Marseille. Au sein de la classe ouvrière, j'ai écrit beaucoup de poèmes qui combattaient cette image de l'Afrique "petit enfant" ou de Peter Pan.*
[I was part of an anti-colonialist group and had, in this context, published several poems in the first issue of *Peuples opprimés*. This was a periodical affiliated with the *Cahiers du Sud* in Marseilles. I wrote many poems within the working-class movement combatting this child-like or Peter Pan-like image of Africa.]

Sada Niang: *Les personnages que vous décrivez dans* Le docker noir *viennent de toutes les parties de l'Afrique . . .*
[One does notice that the characters in *The Black Docker* originate from different parts of Africa . . . .]

Ousmane Sembène: *Ce roman est plus ou moins autobiographique. Le port de Marseille occupait une place très importante dans mon univers à l'époque. J'étais responsable de la CGT (Confédération Générale des Travailleurs) et il gravitait autour de moi des ouvriers qui venaient de partout, des navigateurs surtout. Vous savez, à cette époque, Marseille, Le Havre, Dunkerque représentaient des lieux privilégiés de l'histoire coloniale. Il s'agissait de lieux importants où l'on trouvait des Africains dont les conditions de vie et de lutte différaient radicalement de celles des Africains à Paris. Ce n'est que par la suite que j'ai découvert l'existence de gens tels que Lamine Senghor et autres. Je travaillais uniquement au niveau de navigateurs et d'ouvriers africains, des navigateurs surtout, engagés dans la lutte anti-coloniale.*
[*Black Docker* is more or less autobiographical. At that time, the Marseilles harbor was very important in my life. I was the union steward for the CGT (General Confederation of Workers) and surrounded by workers originating from all over. Most of them were sailors. In that period places like Marseilles, Le Havre, Dunkerque were rallying points of colonial history. In these places, one met Africans whose conditions of living and daily struggles were a radical departure from their counterparts in Paris. It was only later that I came to know people like Lamine Senghor. Indeed, all the organizing I did during that time was done among African sailors and workers, mostly sailors, involved in the anti-colonialist struggle.]

Sada Niang: *Quel rapport aviez-vous avec la langue française à cette époque-là?*
[What was your relation to the French language at that time?]

Ousmane Sembène: *C'était un rapport ambigu. Je voulais l'apprendre mais vite j'ai été renvoyé de l'école. Lorsque plus tard j'ai rencontré Aragon qui, au moment où l'Allemagne voulait imposer sa langue à la France, disait: "Le français c'est ma patrie," je lui ai rétorqué que pour moi c'était mon exil intérieur et extérieur à la fois. C'était une boutade qui m'était venue et que je lui avais lancée pendant que nous militions ensemble au parti communiste. Mais aujourd'hui je me rends compte de l'exactitude de la formule. Pour moi, la langue française est un outil dont je me sers et envers lequel je ne nourris aucun complexe. Certes, à l'époque, je ne m'étais pas encore penché sur le problème linguistique de manière personnelle, mais avant même d'aller en France j'usais quotidiennement de quatre langues en Casamance. Peut-être qu'à l'intérieur de moi même, il n'y avait pas de place pour la langue française. C'était une langue peu utilisée en Casamance dans le commerce quotidien au sein de la population. Et même à Dakar, à l'époque, on utilisait la langue wolof. Le français n'était ni plus ni moins qu'un outil de travail. Je crois qu'il faudrait rendre hommage aux premiers intellectuels sénégalais qui parlaient très bien le wolof. N'oubliez pas qu'à Saint Louis, à l'époque, Le Cid et Les misérables avaient déjà été traduits et déclamés en wolof. Peut-être que la vision de la langue comme élément unificateur de la patrie nous faisait défaut, mais nous avions l'orgueil d'une connaissance profonde de notre langue et la volonté de la développer.*

[My relationship to this language was ambiguous. I wanted to learn it, but was quickly kicked out of school. Later on, when I met Aragon who used to say, at the time when Nazi Germany wanted to impose its own language on France, "The French language is my country," I shot back saying that, for me, it represented both an internal and external exile. It was a witty formula that I threw at him while we were both militants in the Communist Party, but one which, on second thought, is quite to the point. French, for me, is a tool for communication. It is at my disposal and I harbor no inferiority complex towards it. It is true that, at the time, I had not yet positioned myself clearly on the language question. However, even before I left for France, I was daily using up to four languages in the Casamance. Perhaps there was no room left for the French language within myself. French was not often used by the local population in their daily dealings. And even in Dakar, it was Wolof that people used the most. French was no more than a working tool. I think that credit should be given to the first Senegalese intellectuals whose competence in the Wolof language was flawless. Remember that in Saint Louis, at that time, *Le Cid* and *Les misérables* had already been translated and performed in Wolof. We might not have envisioned this language as a patriotic unifying force, but we took pride in a total knowledge of our language, and had the will to develop it further.]

Sada Niang: *Contrairement au* Docker noir, O pays, mon beau peuple *comprend des dialogues directement traduits du wolof. Nous trouvons par exemple cette phrase:*

"Mon frère, je ne te coupe pas le cou, mais . . ." ou cette autre dans les salutations:
"Avez-vous la paix?" Quelle fonction attribuez-vous à ces excrescences wolof dans
un texte français?
[Contrary to *The Black Docker*, *O pays, mon beau peuple* features dialogues which are
literal translations from Wolof to French. I found expressions such as "My brother, I
am not beheading you, but. . ." or "Do you have peace?" How important are these
Wolof presences in a text written in French?]

Ousmane Sembène: *Leur présence est tout à fait normale puisque à l'origine même,*
je ne possédais d'autre registre du français que celle-là. Ensuite, très vite, j'ai
constaté que lorsque les gens lisent ou parlent ils ne reproduisent pas un français de
France ou senghorien mais des expressions directement traduites du wolof, du
bambara ou du pular. J'ai totalement intégré cette pratique. C'est en moi, c'est ma
nature. La majorité des gens au Sénégal ne font que traduire directement l'expression
wolof et tant pis pour ceux qui n'en comprennent pas le sens. Avec l'avènement des
indépendances, il s'est développé par exemple le français de la Côte d'Ivoire qui est
une traduction de diverses langues ivoiriennes. Il ne faut pas oublier, non plus,
l'abâtardissement des diverses langues dans ce creuset que constitue la capitale et qui
a donné naissance à de nombreuses expressions nouvelles. L'auteur qui au Sénégal
a le mieux utilisé le wolof, c'est Birago Diop dans Les contes d'Amadou Koumba. *Un*
lecteur compétent en wolof lisant Birago Diop en français se rendra immédiatement
compte que c'est du wolof traduit qui lui est proposé. Je pense que dès l'enfance,
nombre de nous avions été éduqués dans ce sens. N'oubliez pas que l'époque coloniale
s'est caractérisée par l'occupation des terres et non de l'intérieur des têtes. Chez
nous, c'était notre culture, notre langue qui réglait nos actions quotidiennes. La
langue française, elle, se limitait aux communications avec le dominateur. Ce n'était
pas la langue parlée au sein de la maison, dans la cour ou au marché.
[Their occurrence is unavoidable since, at the beginning, this was the only variety of
French available to me. As well, I very quickly realized that whether they are reading
or speaking, people do not produce a metropolitan or Senghorian French. They use
expressions which are literal translations from Wolof, Bambara or Pular. I have made
this practice mine. It is within me, and has become part of what I am. Most people in
Senegal translate literally from Wolof to French without any regard for those who
cannot grasp the meaning of what they say. In the Ivory Coast for example, a local
variety of French has developed which includes literal translations from various
Ivoirian languages. In addition, one should not forget that in the melting pot of African
capitals, several languages become bastardized and give birth to numerous new
expressions. In Senegal, the writer who has most convincingly used the Wolof is
Birago Diop in his *Les contes d'Amadou Koumba*. Any reader competent in Wolof and
reading Birago Diop will realize that this text is a literal translation from Wolof. I think

that many of us had been educated in this direction. Colonialism took away our lands but not our heads. At home, our daily acts were regulated by our culture. The French language acted as a tool of communication with the dominator. It was not the language we used at home, in the yard or at the market.]

Sada Niang: *Aujourd'hui, la majorité de la population sénégalaise parle et comprend le wolof. Cette langue, de plus en plus, s'annonce comme celle qui pourrait faire l'unité du pays. A votre avis, qu'est-ce qui s'y oppose?*
[Today the majority of the Senegalese society is fluent in Wolof. Wolof, it seems, is carving out itself as the language that could unify the country. What, in your mind, are the factors militating against this?]

Ousmane Sembène: *C'est une situation difficile et délicate à la fois, surtout lorsqu'on ne détient pas le pouvoir de décision. On a cette boutade politique et historique que représente l'assemblée nationale. Lorsque le député Mbaye Niang qui a remplacé Cheikh Anta à l'assemblée nationale y a proposé l'adoption du wolof comme langue nationale, le président en exercice lui a rétorqué: "Moi je suis pular, on va parler pular." Or, suprême contradiction: au sein de cette auguste assemblée, il siège des députés qui ne parlent ni pular ni français bien que le discours officiel s'y déroule en français. Il y a pire: lorsque vous allez devant les tribunaux, les magistrats sont wolof et parlent wolof, les prévenus sont wolof et parlent wolof, mais les gens ne parlent que par des interprètes. Ce que le prévenu dit en wolof, le président, les juges, les assesseurs le comprennent parfaitement, mais malgré tout, il faut que ceci leur soit traduit en français. N'est-ce pas ridicule ça? La solution à ce problème grave relève d'un acte politique pur et simple. Ceci dit, le choix de la langue nationale est devenu un problème délicat. Si nous y étions mis dès l'orée de l'indépendance, la situation aurait été toute autre. Mais aujourd'hui, les gens se regroupent autour de leurs langues. Nous avons par exemple au Sénégal le groupe "alpularen" qui est très dynamique et qui écrit beaucoup en "pular," le groupe xasonké, le groupe soninké, le groupe wolof. Je pense qu'il n'est pas trop tard pour se décider, mais faut-il encore nous laisser assumer nos contradictions et permettre à ces langues de se faire concurrence entre elles. Une décision unilatérale en ce sens pourrait être très lourde de conséquences politiques. Les puissances à l'extérieur peuvent facilement s'instituer en facteur de division pour scinder ces différents groupes. S'agissant du nombre plus grand de locuteurs wolof, on est en droit de se poser la question: pourquoi le wolof est la langue la plus parlée? Il existe plusieurs éléments de réponse: Dakar étant la capitale et une ville côtière, les Wolof et les fils des Wolof ont été les premiers auxiliaires des colonialistes. Ils ont participé à l'esclavage, à la vente. Le roi du Saloum a été le premier à vendre l'île de Saint Louis aux toubabs. Les Wolof ont servi le colon partout, comme subalternes sans se débarrasser de leur propre langue.*

D'autre part, les Wolof ont été les grands missionnaires de la religion musulmane. Il s'est donc créé, dans l'histoire coloniale, un noyau de privilèges au sein de ce groupe. Les gens veulent parler wolof pour s'approcher du pouvoir et de ces noyaux de privilèges. Si le wolof a ce rayonnement aujourd'hui, ce n'est pas à attribuer à sa culture. Actuellement nous assistons à une situation des plus graves: la mort et la disparition progressive de certaines langues. Nous constatons que, de plus en plus, le groupe minoritaire sérère perd sa langue au profit du wolof; nous constatons aussi que les Diola parlent de plus en plus wolof. Par contre nous constatons aussi le développement des langues pular et bambara. Si on prend le secteur de l'Ouest Africain qui s'étend de la Mauritanie à la Côte d'Ivoire, il n'existe pas une seule langue qui couvre cette surface à 50%. Cependant le bambara et le pular restent les deux langues les plus usitées. Le wolof est une langue minoritaire parlée par une portion des huit millions de Sénégalais.

[It is both a difficult and delicate situation, especially when one does not have the power to make decisions. In Senegal, we have this sign of political and historical aberration: the National Assembly. When the Member of Parliament Mbaye Niang (he replaced Cheikh Anta) proposed that Wolof be adopted as the national language, the President (of the National Assembly) replied, "I am of Pular ancestry, let us speak Pular." But there is a blatant contradiction: In this most revered assembly, there are parliamentarians who speak neither Pular, nor French even though the official discourse is conducted in French. Wait, it gets even better: When you go to court, the magistrates are Wolof and speak Wolof, the accused are Wolof and speak Wolof but these two groups only speak through interpreters. Any statement made by the accused in Wolof is fully understood by the presiding judge, the trial judge and the lawyers, but still somebody has to provide French translation for them. Isn't that ridiculous? This is a serious problem which requires bold political action. Having said this, I concur that the selection of the national language has become a delicate problem. Had we tackled it at the very beginning of independence, the situation would have been totally different. But today, people are regrouping around their languages. We now have an active "Alpularen" group which does a lot of writing in Pular, a Xasonké group, a Soninké group and a Wolof group. It may not be too late for a decision, but we should be left to assume our contradictions, and the languages left to compete among themselves. Otherwise, some outside power could very well use this situation and divide the different groups. As to the greater number of Wolof speakers, one may legitimately ask how is it that Wolof is the most used language in the country? There are a few answers: Dakar being a coastal city and the capital, the Wolof and their sons were the first auxiliaries of the colonialists. Furthermore, they took part in the slave trade and the selling of slaves. The king of Saloum was the first monarch to have sold the island of Saint Louis to the Tubabs. The Wolof people have made their services available to the colonial administrators everywhere, have worked under the supervision of the latter while still retaining their language. And besides, the Wolof were the great missionaries of Islam. Thus throughout the colonial history of Africa, there emerged among the Wolof a cluster of people enjoying power and privilege. Others want to speak Wolof to get near the power and privilege enjoyed by these people. The fact that Wolof enjoys such wide influence today is not to be attributed to anything intrinsic to Wolof culture. Furthermore, today we are facing one of the gravest situations: the death and gradual disappearance of some languages. Increasingly, the minority Sérèr group is losing its speakers to Wolof; as well, an increasing number of Diola speak Wolof. However, Bambara and Pular are acquiring more speakers. If you take the region of West Africa going from Mauritania to the Ivory Coast, no one language is spoken by fifty percent of the population, but Bambara and Pular are the two most widely used. Wolof, it turns out, is a minority language spoken by a portion of the eight million Senegalese.]

Sada Niang: *Qu'est-ce que vous aviez voulu faire avec* Kaddu*?*
[What were your objectives when you initiated the periodical *Kaddu*?]

Ousmane Sembène: *Kaddu était un groupement qui cherchait à promouvoir les langues nationales sans privilégier l'une au détriment de l'autre. C'était un mouvement important à l'époque, qui n'a malheureusement pas survécu mais qui comprenait un groupe sérère, pular et évidemment un groupe wolof. Par la suite, ce dernier groupe s'est désagrégé, tandis que le groupe pular a redoublé de dynamisme. Il existe aujourd'hui une contradiction suprême en ce que l'enseignement du wolof est assumé par les Américains et non des Wolof. Je suis actuellement dans un groupe avec un certain M. Tostan et au sein duquel des jeunes enseignent le wolof moyennant un salaire. Cependant, nous nous heurtons à un mur incontournable: que peut-on faire avec la connaissance du wolof? Les langues nationales au Sénégal ne jouissent d'aucun support institutionnel.*
[Kaddu was a group of people who sought to promote the national languages without preferring one over the others. It was an important movement at the time, but unfortunately it did not survive. It included a Sérèr, a Pular and of course a Wolof group. In the end, the Wolof group disintegrated while the Pular one became very dynamic. Today, there is a blatant contradiction in that the Americans, not any Wolof, are teaching the Wolof language in Senegal. I am presently working in a group with a certain M. Tostan. In it, we have young Senegalese people who teach Wolof and who receive a salary. However, we are up against a wall: What can one do with the knowledge of Wolof? National languages in Senegal do not enjoy any institutional support.]

Sada Niang: *On ne vous entend jamais, et on vous voit encore moins sur le circuit de la "francophonie." Pourquoi?*
[You are never heard, let alone seen, on the "francophonie" circuit. Why?]

Ousmane Sembène: *Je ne connais pas la francophonie. C'est quoi au juste? La langue française? On peut parler français, anglais, japonais, wolof. Ce sont des outils de communication. Jamais tu ne seras français au milieu des Français. Ce n'est pas parce que je conduis une voiture Ford, Toyota que je fais partie de la famille Ford ou que je suis japonais. Pour moi, c'est un concept artificiel qui passera tout comme la négritude.*
[I do not know what "francophonie" is. What is it exactly? Is it the French language? Anyone may speak French, English, Japanese, Wolof. These are tools for communicating with each other. Never will you pass for French in the midst of French people. The fact that I drive a Ford or Toyota car will not get me into the Ford family, nor will it make a Japanese out of me, for that matter. For me "francophonie" is an artificial concept which will disappear just as did negritude.]

Sada Niang: *Je sais que vous avez publié le scénario de "Ceddo" en wolof. Je sais aussi qu'à un certain moment de votre carrière d'écrivain, vous avez décidé de ne plus écrire en français et d'adopter le wolof à la place. Cependant,* Niiwam *que vous avez publié tout récemment est écrit en français. Que s'est-il passé entre temps?*
[I know that you published the scenario of "Ceddo" in Wolof, and also that, at some point in your career, you decided to stop writing in French and adopt Wolof instead. Yet *Niiwam*, your last published work, is in French. Did anything happen that made you change your mind?]

Ousmane Sembène: *J'avais pris cette résolution après la publication de* L'Harmattan *mais est-ce vraiment réaliste? Personne ne m'oblige à écrire en wolof, en pular, en bambara ou en français. Puisque le choix existe d'écrire à la fois en français et en wolof pourquoi ne pas adopter les deux codes. Je suis revenu sur ma décision car me limiter exclusivement au wolof m'aurait occasionné des endettements inutiles.*
[I had made that decision after *L'Harmattan* was published. But how realistic was it? Nobody forces me to write in Wolof, Pular, Bambara or French. Since I have the choice of writing in French and Wolof, why not adopt both these codes? I changed my mind because limiting myself to Wolof would have resulted in huge debts for no purpose.]

Sada Niang: *Que pensez-vous de la décision de Ngugi wa Thiong'o qui refuse la création littéraire en anglais?*
[What do you think of a writer like Ngugi wa Thiong'o who rejects any literary creation in English?]

Ousmane Sembène: *J'ai rencontré Ngugi il y a deux ans dans le Massachussetts. Concernant sa position je dois dire que je suis d'accord avec lui. Cependant, l'acte révolutionnaire ne doit pas être un frein. Si l'artiste s'enferme et n'a pas de quoi vivre, il ne peut pas travailler. Si j'écrivais en wolof, ce serait tout à mon honneur, mais qui me lirait? Les moyens de communication et de distribution de cette littérature sont contrôlés par un gouvernement. Si ce gouvernement ne fait rien pour les langues nationales, que puis-je faire à mon niveau personnel? Actuellement, il existe au Sénégal un Ministère de langues et d'alphabétisation qui en fait moins que Tostan à Thiès. Mes livres sont traduits en wolof pour les paysans et en attendant, j'écris en wolof en petit noyau.*

[I met Ngugi two years ago at the Conference in Massachussetts. I agree with his position but I do not think that the revolutionary act should be a limitation. The artist who closes himself in, and does not have a livelihood cannot work. If I wrote in Wolof, it would all be to my credit, but who would read me? The means of communication and distribution of our literature are controlled by a government. If this body does nothing for the national languages, what can I do at my own level? At the moment there is a ministry of languages and literacy promotion in Senegal which is less active than M. Tostan in Thiès. My books are translated into Wolof for the peasants; in the meantime, I am writing in Wolof in a small group.]

Sada Niang: *Avez-vous visionné un film comme "Ceddo," en wolof, dans les campagnes sénégalaises?*
[Did you screen "Ceddo," in Wolof, in rural areas in Senegal?]

Ousmane Sembène: *Oui!*
[I did!]

Sada Niang: *Quel était la réaction de ce public?*
[What was the reaction of this audience?]

Ousmane Sembène: *Il y a eu des discussions très animées. "Ceddo" est un film à réflexion dans lequel j'ai essayé de montrer comment la religion musulmane a pénétré chez nous, ce qu'elle a voulu accomplir et le substrat culturel qui en reste aujourd'hui. Nous avons beau être musulmans ou catholiques, notre substrat culturel reste néanmoins profondément ancré dans ce monde des ceddo. Et cela, c'est très important. Ceci veut dire que notre culture est encore très vivante, très forte. Nous pouvons absorber les autres, les utiliser et nous adapter sans rien perdre. Au Sénégal, on a des chefs religieux, des chefs traditionnels et des députés. Il existe une administration héritée de l'époque coloniale mais celle-ci ne peut survivre sans les imams; d'autre part à côté de ce chef religieux on trouvera toujours un chef traditionnel gardien de* *la tradition. Quand bien même les représentants de ces trois niveaux sont tous musulmans, ces distinctions existent nettement. Faut-il voir en ceci le signe d'une contradiction ou d'un dynamisme qui nous échappe? Car ce qui est valable chez les Wolof l'est aussi pour les Bambara, les Toucouleur et ailleurs en Afrique.*

[There were very heated debates. "Ceddo" is a thought-provoking movie. In it I attempted to show how Islam penetrated Senegal, what this religion tried to accomplish and the cultural substratum that is still with us today. Despite the fact that we are Muslim or Christian, we remain deeply rooted in the universe of the *ceddo*. This is of paramount importance; for it means that our culture is very much alive, very strong. We can absorb other cultures, use them, adapt ourselves without any loss. In Senegal you have religious chiefs, traditional chiefs and members of the National Assembly. There is a colonial administration inherited from the colonial era, but this administration cannot survive without the "imams"; furthermore beside this religious chief, you will always find a traditional chief guarding the tradition. These are clear distinctions, even if the representatives of the three levels are all Muslim. Is this the sign of a contradiction or the manifestation of a dynamic system whose workings elude us? For what is valid for the Wolof is also valid for the Bambara, the Toucouleur and anybody else in Africa.]

Sada Niang: *Est-ce que cette situation ne signifie pas une impossibilité de se débarrasser de l'un ou de l'autre de ces trois niveaux?*
[Perhaps none of these levels can be done without?]

Ousmane Sembène: *Ça, je ne le sais et ce n'est pas à moi de le dire! Il faudrait laisser les choses évoluer d'elles-mêmes.*
[That I do not know and it is not up to me to say. I think that things should be left alone and allowed to find their own progression.]

Sada Niang: *Vous a-t-on jamais demandé de changer le style d'un passage de vos textes pour refléter un usage plus standard, plus "normal"?*
[Were you ever asked to alter the style of a passage in one of your texts so as to reflect a more "standard" usage?]

Ousmane Sembène: *L'éditeur est un écrivain raté. J'ai toujours eu mon indépendance et mes textes sont à prendre ou à laisser. Il existe des maisons d'édition où les prouesses de la langue dominent sur tout. Ceci convient peut-être aux écrivains tels Senghor, mais moi, je ne peux pas être un produit parfait du système colonial.*
[An editor is an unsuccessful writer. I have always had my freedom and my texts are to be taken as is or left alone. There are publishing houses where linguistic virtuosity

ranks above everything else. This may do for writers like Senghor. As for me, I find it impossible to be the perfect product of the colonial system.]

Sada Niang: *Ousmane Sembène, une analyse de vos oeuvres tant cinématographiques que littéraires révèle que vos personnages les plus convaincants fonctionnent sur le mode du refus. Dans "La noire de . . .," Diouanna se suicide plutôt que de se livrer à la servitude; dans "Mandabi," ce sont les femmes de Dieng qui refusent de se faire engloutir par des profiteurs de toutes sortes; dans "Ceddo," la princesse Dior, malgré ses origines sociales refuse de légitimer la domination religieuse. Enfin dans "Camp de Thiaroye" les tirailleurs refusent le mensonge colonial et l'indignité. Quelle valeur attribuez-vous à cette notion de refus?*

[Ousmane Sembène, it seems that your work, whether films, novels or short stories stage characters who become most convincing when they refuse or reject an injustice. In "Black Girl" Diouanna chooses suicide over servitude; in "Mandabi," it is Dieng's wives who refuse to be taken in by all kinds of profiteers; in "Ceddo," Princess Dior, in spite of her aristocratic origins, refuses to give legitimacy to religious oppression; and finally in "Camp de Thiaroye" the Senegalese infantrymen refuse to be taken in by the old colonial lies and indignities. How important is the notion of "refusal" for you?]

Ousmane Sembène: *Il existe toujours dans une situation donnée des personnages qui refusent. On ne peut pas dire que tout un peuple a accepté ou refusé, mais je type mes personnages et ce sont là des personnages que je comprends bien. Il y a des choses que l'on ne peut pas accepter. L'homme n'est grand que dans la mesure où il refuse ces choses pour s'assumer. De fait, quand l'homme refuse, c'est qu'il s'assume, car ce que tu refuses, tu dois le conquérir ailleurs par ta propre force. Quelques cinq ou dix années après l'indépendance, on nous a accoutumés à l'assistance, à l'aide, n'est-ce pas humiliant? On ne peut pas s'assumer en tendant la main toute sa vie durant. Kocc Barma disait: "Soo bugéé rey goor, subë guné dékoy défal lumu bëgg, su yaggé, ab dakk ngey am" ("Si tu veux détruire un honnête homme, exauce ses désirs tous les jours. Enfin de compte, il deviendra comme un cerf") et aussi "Soo amé xarit, loo wax muné degglë, amoo xarit, jaam nga am" ("Un ami qui approuve tout ce que tu dis n'est point un ami mais un esclave"). Nous sommes tellement habitués à l'aide que vous qui vivez à l'extérieur êtes aussi humiliés. A chaque fois que se présente un chef d'état africain, la presse se demande: "Combien a-t-il ramassé?" et pour nous humilier davantage on trouvera dans cette même presse: "Tel chef d'état est arrivé mais on ne lui a rien apporté comme aide." De tout temps, le refus a été le signe d'une dignité fondamentale. Je ne sais pas si vous connaissez ce poème wolof: "Am yalla joxla silmaxa, munéla gacc gënu mala ka gis, defko ci" ("Indigent, prends cette aumône,* *et mets-la dans ton écuelle, pour la grâce de dieu." Il te répond: "Honte à toi, tu vois aussi bien que moi, dépose-la donc toi-même"). Il s'agit d'un mendiant qui refuse l'humiliation. Vous savez que dans la tradition africaine, les hommes ont pendant longtemps refusé la mendicité. "Amna ñoo xamne du:u lekk sarax" ("Il y a des gens qui refusent de manger toute nourriture donnée en aumône"). Je connais de ces familles où l'aumône représente une très grave offense. Il existe aussi ce proverbe wolof que les gens lancent en public: "Su féékééné li ma wax amul, yalla na yelwaan ci sama kanamu nawlé!" ("Si j'ai menti, plût au ciel que je sois obligé de mendier devant mes pairs!"). Maintenant, tous nos états sont pourris.*

[In a given situation, there will always be characters who will say no. It would not be accurate to say that a whole people accepted or refused, but I work with types of characters and I am very sympathetic with those who refuse. Some things are simply not to be accepted. Human beings reach greatness only to the extent that they refuse these things and assume themselves. In fact, when a human being refuses, he/she takes charge of himself/herself. For what you reject in one place will have to be conquered elsewhere with your own strength. Some five to ten years after independence, we became habituated to being assisted through aid programs. How humiliating! One cannot take charge of oneself while extending one's arm from birth to death. Kocc Barma used to say, "Soo bugéé rey goor, subë guné dékoy défal lumu bëgg, su yaggé, ab dakk ngey am" ("If you want to destroy an honorable man, grant him his wishes every single day. In the end, you will turn him into a deer") and again "Soo amé xarit, loo wax muné degglë, amoo xarit, jaam nga am" ("A friend who says yes to everything you say is not a friend but a slave"). We are so used to being assisted that even those of you living outside of Senegal are also humiliated. Whenever an African head of state comes around here, the newspapers ask: "How much did he manage to scoop?" and to humiliate us further, you read in these same newspapers, "Such and such head of state was around but he did not receive any aid package." Since the dawn of times, refusal has been a sign of fundamental dignity. You may know this Wolof adage: "Am yalla joxla silmaxa, munéla gacc gënu mala ka gis, defko ci" ("'Take this alm in the name of God and put it in your bowl, pauper,' and the pauper responds, 'Shame on you, your eyes are just as good as mine, put it in yourself'"). It talks about a beggar who refuses to be humiliated. You know that in the African tradition, people have refused to beg for a long time. "Amna ñoo xamne duñu lekk sarax" ("There are people who would not eat any food obtained through begging"). I know families where receiving alms from somebody is considered a serious offense. You may also know this Wolof proverb often uttered in front of others: "Su féékééné li ma wax amul, yalla na yelwaan ci sama kanamu nawlé!" ("If my words are not true, may I go out begging in front of my peers"!). Today, all our states have been corrupted to the core.]

Sada Niang: *Dans ce cas comment interprétez-vous la recrudescence de la mendicité* *dans les villes africaines?*

[How then do you interpret the increasing number of beggars in African cities?]

Ousmane Sembène: *Ceci relève de la faillite d'une politique. On pourrait aussi parler du chômage, de la famine, de la prostitution. Quand j'ai fait "Mandabi" et "Xala" j'ai eu toutes sortes de problèmes avec la censure. Il suffit de se promener à Dakar, à Abidjan, au Caire pour se rendre compte de la situation. Dans tout le continent on est humilié en tant qu'être humain. Pendant les quelques jours que j'ai été ici, plusieurs personnes sont venues me trouver pour me demander: "Comment pourrais-je vous être utile." Mais basta! Je ne suis pas venu ici pour mendier! Que font ces gens, ils vont dans leur groupe pour dire: "Nous apprenons aux femmes africaines à faire le mil, à coudre, etc." Cela m'irrite . . .! La réalité est que les gouvernements africains ne sont même pas capables d'envoyer infirmiers et médecins travailler dans nos campagnes. Ces mêmes gouvernements disent aux paysans: "Il faut doubler la culture de l'arachide." Ces derniers doublent la culture; les prix baissent! Tous ces problèmes se lient. L'artiste le perçoit et l'évoque, mais ne peut guère offrir de solution.*

[These are the result of bankrupt policies. We may as well talk about unemployment, famine and prostitution. After I shot "Mandabi" and "Xala," I experienced all kinds of difficulties with censorship. Today one only has to take a walk through Dakar, Abidjan, Cairo to realize what is happening: throughout the continent, we are being humiliated as human beings. During the few days that I have been here, several persons have come to me with this question: "What can I do to help you?" Basta! I have not come here to beg. And what do such people do? They go around to their groups and tell how they teach African women to grind millet, to sew, etc. I find this very irritating . . .! The real issue is that our governments are not even able to send nurses and doctors into the rural areas. These same governments will tell peasants, "Double your peanut production." The peasants comply and immediately the prices drop. All these problems are related. The artist perceives them and describes them without being able to offer a solution.]

Sada Niang: *Pourquoi ce refus se manifeste-t-il dans sa puissance absolue chez vos personnages féminins?*

[Why is the notion of refusal most strongly expressed by your female characters?]

Ousmane Sembène: *C'est toujours les hommes qui vont en guerre, mais qui assume l'éducation des enfants, l'entretien des cultures, la protection des animaux et du cheptel, qui pile? Ce sont les femmes. L'Afrique ne se développera pas sans la participation concrète de la femme. La conception que nos pères avaient de la femme doit être enterrée une fois pour toutes. La femme est l'élément le plus solide d'une* *communauté, d'une société. C'est pour elle qu'on crée ce qu'il y a de plus beau. Il faut par exemple entendre ces poèmes pular consacrés aux boeufs. Le boeuf est un animal tellement joli; il est toujours comparé à la femme. Par contre, dans les poèmes wolof, il en existe très peu consacrés aux femmes. La culture africaine n'est pas homogène. En fait, je dirais même que le Sénégal n'a pas de culture. Aujourd'hui, les différents groupes ethniques qui composent le pays sont en train de vallonner, de s'interpénétrer pour créer une nouvelle culture. Ce collage, la somme de toutes ces différences aboutira à une culture sénégalaise géographiquement parlant. Aujourd'hui, tout le monde vit une situation économique identique, mais des cultures différentes.*

[Men are always the ones to go to war. But who looks after the education of children, who raises the crops, who cares for the cattle, who does the grinding of the grain? It is women who perform these tasks. The development of Africa will not happen without the effective participation of women. Our forefathers' image of women must be buried once for all. Women are the most solid component of a community, of a society. It is for women that the highest beauty is created. You should hear the Pular poems composed to celebrate cattle. These are such beautiful animals; they are always being compared to women. However, there are very few poems celebrating women among the Wolof. Homogeneity of African culture is nothing more than a myth. I will even go so far as to say that we do not have a homogeneous culture in Senegal. At present the different ethnic groups that make up Senegal are in the process of interpenetration, of levelling out, and creating a new culture. The collage that is the sum of all the differences between them will lead to a culture that geographically speaking we can call Senegalese. As it is today, all the population lives in the same economic situation but in different cultures.]

Sada Niang: *Pourquoi Dieng refuse-t-il de vendre sa maison dans "Mandabi" alors qu'il accepte toutes les autres humiliations mesquines des autres?*

[In "Mandabi," Dieng silently accepts all kinds of humiliations but enters into a great fit of anger when he is asked to sell his house. Where does the energy of such refusal come from?]

Ousmane Sembène: *Il refuse, car l'homme peut tout perdre sauf d'assumer sa responsabilité de père de famille. La vente de la maison annoncerait sa chute fatale, sa mort. Dieng appartient à une autre génération wolof. Pour lui comme pour moi, il n'est pas question de vendre sa maison. "Kër sa kër laa" ("La demeure familiale est inaliénable"). Or maintenant, nous entrons dans une période moderne où le "kër" est devenu un bien immobilier. Dieng habitait une petite cahutte. Si c'était un goinfre, il aurait vendu sa maison pour résoudre la situation dramatique dans laquelle il se trouve. Dieng est un prototype pas plus. J'ai connu un homme qui a vécu cette même expérience. Tout dernièrement la même situation s'est reproduite avec les travailleurs* *immigrés qui envoyaient de l'argent à leurs familles dans la région du Sénégal Oriental. Si bien qu'aujourd'hui, ces travailleurs préfèrent payer le voyage à l'un des leurs qui viendra faire la distribution à leurs familles au Sénégal. A un moment donné l'état sénégalais lui-même était incapable d'honorer les mandats. J'ai présenté "Mandabi" l'an passé dans la série de mes projections foraines, j'ai discuté avec des jeunes et ils m'ont dit: "Nous n'avons jamais entendu parler de ce film mais nous pouvons dire qu'il vient juste d'être filmé." Je me suis dit: "Mais ce n'est pas possible, cela n'a pas changé, c'est pire." La semaine suivante, je leur ai projeté "Xala." Ils m'ont dit: "Mais enfin c'est la suite de 'Mandabi,' c'est encore pire!" C'est avec mon prochain film que j'aurai terminé le cycle des films sur l'évolution de l'Afrique.*

[He refuses to do so because a man may fail everywhere except when it comes to his duty as a head of the family. Selling the house would herald a fatal downfall, his death. Dieng belongs to a different Wolof generation. For him just as for me, selling one's house is out of the question. "Kër sa kër laa" ("One's home is one's home"). But today, we have entered an era where a "kër"—a home—has been turned into a real estate commodity. Dieng's house was just a small wooden structure. Had he been a greedy person, he would have sold it to resolve the disastrous situation in which he found himself. He is only a prototype. I knew a man who lived a similar experience. Recently, a similar situation happened with the Senegalese migrant workers in France. They would send money to their families in Sénégal Oriental, but it would never get there. Today these workers prefer to pay the airfare of one of them who comes and distributes the money to their families. There was a time when even the Senegalese state was unable to honor the money orders. Last year, I showed "Mandabi" during one of my rural screenings. Later on, I had some discussions with the young people and they told me, "We had never heard of this film, but we know that it has just been shot." I said to myself, "My God, this is impossible! Nothing has changed. It has gotten worse." The following week, I brought them "Xala" and they said, "This is the sequel to 'Mandabi,' it's even worse." With my next film, I will have finished the series of films on the evolution of Africa.]

Sada Niang: *Quel est votre rapport à l'histoire en tant qu'artiste? Je pense ici surtout à "Camp de Thiaroye."*

[How do you define your relationship with history. I am particularly thinking of "Camp de Thiaroye."]

Ousmane Sembène: *L'artiste est là pour révéler un certain nombre de faits historiques que l'on voudrait taire. De tous temps, on a eu les "mbandkat" ("un artiste de variétés"), les conteurs, les "baruwaan," et autres. La société wolof a toujours eu des gens qui sont là pour évoquer, rappeler et projeter vers quelque chose.*

[The artist is here to reveal a certain number of historical facts that others would like to keep hidden. Since the dawn of time, we have had people like the "mbandkat" ("a performer in variety shows"), the storytellers, the "baruwaan," and others. Wolof society has always had people whose role it was to give voice, bring back to memory, and project toward something.]

Sada Niang: *Dans "Emitaï," vous abordez le thème de l'exaction de l'impôt de guerre. . .*
[In "Emitaï," you explore the theme of the war tax. . .]

Ousmane Sembène: *J'ai une note très intéressante sur la manière dont l'impôt a été introduit chez les Africains. J'ai donné une conférence sur ce sujet à la banque, mais ils étaient très embarrassés. L'impôt annuel existait déjà chez nous, mais en nature et non en espèces. Pour créer l'impôt en espèces, Archinard a calculé l'équivalent de la redevance en noix de cola, en animaux et en or. Savez-vous ce qu'on allait faire de la cola en 1886-1887? Qu'est-ce que les blancs allaient faire de la cola? Eh bien, cette période a coïncidé à la fabrication du Coca-Cola. Le consul des Etats-Unis au Sénégal qui résidait à la Sierra Léone est venu au Sénégal. En échange de cette cola, les Etats-Unis ont donné du corned beef à Archinard. Cette cola a servi à l'une des premières fabrications du Coca-Cola. Le corned beef qui était ainsi échangé venait de Chicago, de Kansas en passant par la France. L'armée coloniale a utilisé ce corned beef lors de la conquête du Soudan vers 1890. Le colonel Baratier en fait une description détaillée dans ses documents. Et c'est à partir de cette description que je suis allé à Washington au département d'état pour retrouver le modèle de la boîte. La recherche est une nécessité absolue pour nous.*
[I have an interesting footnote on how taxes were introduced in Africa. I even gave a lecture on that topic at the bank, but it embarrassed them considerably. The collection of annual taxes already existed in Africa. But these were paid in kind, not in cash. When Archinard created the notion of taxes to be paid in cash, he calculated the equivalent of the amount due in cola nuts, in cattle and in gold. Now, do you know what they were going to do with cola nuts in 1886-1887? What could white people use cola nuts for? Well, this period coincided with the fabrication of Coca-Cola. The Consul of the United States who then resided in Sierra Leone came to Senegal and, in exchange for these cola nuts, the United States gave corned beef tins to Archinard. Those nuts were used for one of the first productions of Coca-Cola. The corned beef provided in exchange came from Chicago and Kansas via France. Around 1890, during the conquest of the Sudan, the French colonial army was fed on that corned beef. Colonel Baratier gives a detailed description of this in his archives. And from this description, I was able to go to the State Department in Washington and find a replica of the original tin box. Research is an absolute necessity for us.]

Sada Niang: *Ousmane Sembène, le thème de l'esclavage revient très souvent dans votre oeuvre. On pense à "La noire de . . .," à "Voltaïque," et à "Ceddo." Dans "Camp de Thiaroye," par le biais d'un personnage afro-américain, vous établissez le lien entre la situation sociale du colonisé et celle des Afro-américains. Enfin, lors du visionnenment de ce film à Toronto, vous avez dit haut et net: "Jamais plus jamais, je ne serai l'esclave de personne." Quel sens donnez-vous à l'esclavage?*

[Ousmane Sembène, slavery is an important issue in your work. I am thinking of "La noire de . . .," "Voltaïque" and "Ceddo." In "Camp de Thiaroye" you stage an African-American character as a way of mirroring the situation of the colonized against that of the African American. Finally, after the showing of this film in Toronto, you stated loud and clear to a packed audience: "Never ever will I be anybody's slave again." What is the meaning of slavery for you?]

Ousmane Sembène: *Nous avons été les premiers esclavagistes. Dès qu'il y avait une guerre, les membres du groupe ou de la communauté vaincue étaient transformés en esclaves. Ces esclaves sont restés des domestiques jusqu'au moment où "les Walo Walo" (les habitants du Walo) après avoir vendu les terrains ont commencé à vendre les gens. L'esclavage traditionnel diffère de la traite en ce que cette dernière se fondait sur la monnaie et le profit. Traditionnellement, les esclaves avaient un délégué qui participait aux discussions lors des palabres, et parfois même celui-ci était très près du roi. L'esclave est devenu valeur marchande avec l'attrait de l'or, des pacotilles, du vin. C'est ainsi qu'en wolof nous avons le terme "jarbaat" qui désigne l'enfant de ta soeur.*

[We were the first slavers. Whenever there was a war, members of the defeated group or community were enslaved. These slaves remained domestics until the moment when, after having sold the land, the "Walo" (the people from the Walo region) decided to sell the people. Traditional slavery differs from the slave trade in that the slave trade was based on money and profit. Traditionally the slaves had a representative who participated in the debates during the community meetings. Sometimes the representative was even very close to the king. Slaves became a commercial commodity with the desire to acquire gold, gadgetry and alcohol. Thus in Wolof there exists the term "jarbaat" which refers to one's sister's child.]

Sada Niang: *Oui, "jardibaat" (Mot à mot: Une personne dont la voix ou le cou a été vendu. Le "jarbaat" hérite de l'oncle à la mort de ce dernier).*

[Yes, "jardibaat" (Literally someone whose neck or voice has been sold. The "jarbaat" normally inherits from his/her uncle when the latter dies.)]

Ousmane Sembène: *Le "jarbaat" pouvait être vendu par l'oncle pour racheter sa propre liberté. Par la suite a eu lieu la chasse, comme dans "Ceddo," comme dans "Voltaïque." Quiconque possédait un fusil pouvait se livrer à la chasse aux esclaves* *pour les déporter. Les blancs ne pénétraient pas à l'intérieur. En 1894 ou 1896, au moment où Samori fuyait vers Bandama, il y avait un marché d'esclaves derrière la maison de Maurice Delafosse. Delafosse ne vendait pas, mais regardait les autres vendre. Il fait une description très détaillée de ce marché d'esclaves dans ses documents. Samori venait là et y échangeait des esclaves parmi les Allemands, les Anglais et les Français. Nous n'en parlons pas souvent mais nous connaissons en wolof les expressions de "Jaamu gééj" (mot à mot: "esclave emmené sur les mers"), "bambara gééj" (mot à mot: "les Bambara de la mer ou emmenés par la mer"). Nous avons pratiqué l'esclavage. La maison des esclaves qui existe actuellement à Gorée appartenait à une famille de métis de Saint Louis: les Crespin. Nous avons même été chercher des esclaves pour qu'ils soient exportés. Il faut que nous ayons le courage de dire ça.*

[The "jarbaat" could be sold by his/her uncle in exchange for the uncle's own freedom. Later on, slaves were hunted down just as in "Ceddo," just as in "Voltaïque." Whoever owned a gun could hunt down slaves and have them deported. The white traders would not go into the hinterland. In 1894 or 1896, while Samori was fleeing towards Bandama, there was a slave market just behind Maurice Delafosse's house. Delafosse never took part in the selling, but would look on while others did the selling. He describes this market in detail in his documents. Samori would come there to trade slaves with the Germans, the British and the French. We do not talk about it frequently, but in Wolof we know the expressions: "Jaamu gééj" (literally "one or (several) slave(s) taken away on the seas"), "bambara gééj" (literally "the Bambara taken out on the seas"). We took part in the slave trade. The "house of slaves" in Gorée used to belong to a mixed-blood family from Saint Louis: the Crespins. We even hunted down slaves so that they could be deported. We should be courageous enough to say it.]

Sada Niang: *Quelle fonction attribuez-vous au personnage du tirailleur?*
[What is the role of the Senegalese infantryman in your work?]

Ousmane Sembène: *Pour comprendre ce personnage, il faut remonter à la période de l'esclavage. Pensez aux "lapto" (veut dire: "interpréter"), "laptokat" (veut dire: "un ou des interprètes"). Dès la soi-disante abolition de l'esclavage, certains détenteurs d'esclaves noirs les ont revendus aux colons, surtout à l'armée. Ces anciens esclaves ont formé le premier corps constitué de militaires. Les tirailleurs font partie de l'histoire coloniale. Par la suite obligation était faite aux rois d'envoyer un contingent donné de tirailleurs. Tirailleurs et école ont constitué un supplément du pouvoir colonial. Je me rappelle une phrase très célèbre d'Archinard qui disait en 1888: "Il faut nommer des chefs noirs à condition de mettre un chef blanc au dessus d'eux car la présence du blanc est très salvatrice au milieu des nègres." Les tirailleurs pouvaient accéder jusqu'au grade de lieutenant ou capitaine mais pas plus. La plupart* *d'entre eux étaient sergents. Le plus célèbre de tous fut un indigène du nom de Al Xamisa dépêché par Galliéni auprès de Samori et qui fut le premier à prendre contact avec ce dernier. On connaît aussi un certain Racine Sy qui devint capitaine dans ce corps de tirailleurs. Il y avait certes parmi eux des évolués car l'école des otages qui par la suite devint l'école des fils de chefs était une pépinière de recrutement pour l'armée coloniale. C'est parmi ceux-ci que se choisissait le chef des indigènes au-dessus duquel était placé un blanc. Ces "cadres" avaient le privilège de pouvoir porter des casques, ce qui leur donnait l'illusion d'être des blancs. Dans l'armée coloniale, les citoyens français revendiquaient le port du casque. Aujourd'hui le casque a disparu, est-ce que le soleil s'est adouci entre temps? Qu'est-ce qui a changé? (Il rit). C'est un sujet passionnant sur lequel j'ai fait des recherches pour "Camp de Thiaroye" et "Samori."*

[To understand this character, you should go back to slavery. Think of "lapto" ("to interpret"), "laptokat" ("one (or several) interpreter(s)"). As early as the so-called abolition of slavery, some slave owners sold their slaves to the colonists, mostly to the colonial army. These former slaves constituted the first military regiment in the colonial army. Later on, each (African) king was required to send a contingent of infantrymen. These infantrymen, along with the introduction of schools, acted as complementary elements to colonial power. I still remember this sentence by Archinard who in 1888 said, "We should appoint black chiefs, provided we also appoint a white chief to oversee them, for the presence of a white man in the midst of blacks is salutary." These infantrymen could be promoted to the rank of lieutenant or captain, but most of them went only as far as sergeants. The most famous of them was a certain Al Xamisa dispatched to Samori by Galliéni, and who was the first man to get in contact with Samori. We also know of a Racine Sy who became captain in the contingent of Senegalese infantrymen. Among them, there were some "évolués" (Europeanized Africans) since the "école des otages" (School for hostages) which became the "école des fils de chefs" (School for the sons of chiefs) acted as a nursery for the colonial army. It was among the graduates of this school that the black chiefs to be supervised by the whites were selected. These "cadres" used to wear helmets, which gave them the illusion of passing as whites. In the colonial army, French citizens made it a point to wear a helmet. Today, the helmet has disappeared; has the sun become weaker over time? (He laughs). This is a fascinating topic on which I did some research for "Camp de Thiaroye" and "Samori."]

Sada Niang: *Dans "Niaye" ce personnage est un personnage dynamique qui débloque l'impasse de la société traditionnelle.*

[In "Niaye," you paint the infantryman as a dynamic character who resolves the impasse in which the traditional society finds itself.]

Ousmane Sembène: *C'était un fou. C'est un personnage qui a fait la guerre du Viet Nam, la campagne d'Indochine. Il ne faut pas non plus négliger l'influence des guerres. Dans mon cas personnel, avant la guerre, je n'avais aucune notion du colonialisme. Je vivais comme un enfant, heureux dans ma brousse. Le blanc m'importait peu. J'avais mon propre univers culturel. Le cinéma était mon seul échappatoire. J'en étais fasciné, mais pas mon père. Je me rappelle que quand nous revenions de la pêche, mon père me donnait des sous pour aller au cinéma. A Ziguinchor, il y avait une route principale sur laquelle se trouvait la salle de cinéma et lorsque je passais devant avec mon père, je m'y arrêtais pour regarder les affiches. Je pense que mon père n'a jamais été au cinéma. Il me demandait tout le temps: "Pourquoi tu vas voir ces 'conneries' de blanc?" C'est dire que quand je grandissais, je n'avais aucune notion de la colonisation. Il a fallu les guerres. Nous devrions étudier l'apport des deux guerres sur la prise de conscience et j'aborde le sujet dans* Le dernier de l'Empire. *C'est lors de la guerre 1914-1918 que nombre de citoyens sénégalais ont revendiqué le droit d'aller à la guerre. La guerre 1939-1945 a bouleversé le monde surtout pour nous. En allant à la guerre on s'est rendu compte que l'homme qui nous faisait peur était nu comme nous, surtout après l'expérience des lâchetés et des bassesses les plus atroces en Europe. Car si chez nous, les noirs ont collaboré avec les esclavagistes, les Français, chez eux, ont collaboré avec l'Allemagne. C'est eux qui ont dénoncé les Juifs, qui les faisaient déporter. Comme on l'a dit dans* "Camp de Thiaroye," *ils arrachaient les dents en or de la bouche des Juifs morts.*

[The character is mad. He had taken part in the war in Viet Nam. One should not underestimate the importance of wars. Personally, before the war, I had no idea of what colonialism was. I lived an innocent life, happy in my bush, in my own cultural universe. The white man was irrelevant to me. The movies were my only escape. I was fascinated by them, but not my father. I remember that on our way back from a day's fishing, he would give me some change to go to the movies. In Ziguinchor, there was a main street with the movie theater on it and I would stop to look at the posters. I do not think that my father ever went to the movies. He would always ask me, "Why do you like going to see these stupidities of the whites?" Indeed, as I was growing up, I had no idea of what colonization was. It took the wars for that. I think that the effect of the two wars on the raising of our consciousness should be studied. I deal with the topic in *The Last of the Empire*. In 1914-1918, a number of Senegalese demanded the right to fight in the war. The 1939-1945 war turned the world upside down, especially ours. During the war, we realized that the man who used to scare us was as naked as we, especially after we witnessed the cowardice and contemptible behavior in Europe. For if in Africa the blacks collaborated with the slavers, in France, the French collaborated with Germany. They informed against the Jews and had them deported. As is mentioned in "Camp de Thiaroye," they would also break the gold teeth out of the mouths of dead Jews.]

Sada Niang: *Il y avait une déperdition morale totale qui a favorisé une prise de conscience de la part des colonisés.*
[There was a total moral downfall that helped to raise the consciousness of the colonized.]

Ousmane Sembène: *Oui. Il y avait aussi un flux révolutionnaire mondial depuis 1917. Vers les années 1922-1923, le panafricanisme se développe. En France, j'ai eu le privilège de rencontrer Ho Chi Minh qui m'a donné à lire ses livres. Avant de lire le* Discours sur le colonialisme *de Césaire, il faudrait lire Ho Chi Minh. J'ai aussi rencontré Chou En Laï, Du Bois, Padmore, et Nkrumah. C'est là les membres d'une génération qui ont fait beaucoup de travail et qui déjà revendiquaient l'indépendance des pays africains bien avant Lamine Guèye, Blaise Diagne et Ngalandu Diouf.*
[Yes. But there was also a world-wide revolutionary surge starting in 1917. Pan-Africanism developed around 1922-1923. In France, I had the good fortune of meeting Ho Chi Minh who gave me his books to read. Before reading Césaire's *Discourse on Colonialism* one should read Ho Chi Minh. I also met Chou En Lai, Du Bois, Padmore, and Nkrumah. The members of that generation did a lot of work and were already protesting for the independence of African countries, even before Lamine Guèye, Blaise Diagne and Ngalandu Diouf.]

Sada Niang: *Pouvez-vous nous dire sur quoi vous travaillez en ce moment?*
[What are you working on at the moment?]

Ousmane Sembène: *Je viens de finir un film encore sur le "refus" intitulé "Gelwaar," je suis en train de finir le roman sur "Gelwaar" qui doit sortir l'année prochaine, et je suis en train d'adapter* Le dernier de l'Empire *au cinéma. J'ai commencé ce dernier travail en 1981, le jour du départ de Senghor, le jour de sa succession par Abdou Diouf. Je pense que c'est une veine que je vais terminer ma série sur l'Afrique pour montrer le prix à payer pour la démocratie. La démocratie c'est une sorte de "nawlanté" (approximativement: "entretenir avec ses pairs des rapports d'égalité imbue d'un profond sens de l'honneur") du moins dans le discours. En fait il ne peut pas y avoir de démocratie dans la pauvreté. S'il y a une minorité de riches et une majorité de pauvres, il n'y a pas de démocratie. Cependant cette minorité de riches peut manipuler la majorité de pauvres pour créer une démocratie et l'Occident y verra clair puisque nous aurons le droit d'expression et d'oppression aussi.*
[I just completed another film, "Gelwaar," again on the theme of "refusal." I am completing the novel on "Gelwaar" which should come out next year, and I am adapting *The Last of the Empire* to the screen. This last project was started the day Senghor resigned in 1981, the day Abdou Diouf took over. I think I am lucky to be finishing my series on Africa which shows the price to be paid for democracy.

Democracy is a kind of "nawlanté" (approximately: "dealing with one's peers with fairness and a deep sense of honor") at least on the level of discourse; in practice, there can be no democracy in poverty. If you have a minority of rich people and a majority of poor people, there can be no democracy. However, this minority of rich people can manipulate the majority of poor people to create a democratic regime. The West gets what it bargained for, since we will have acquired the right to express ourselves and oppress others!]

Sada Niang: *Ousmane Sembène, Merci!*
[Ousmane Sembène, thank you.]

NOTES

[1] In this article we refer to the following editions of works by Ousmane Sembène: *Le docker noir* (Paris: Présence Africaine, 1973; first edition: Paris: Debresse, 1956); *0 pays, mon beau peuple* (Paris: Presses Pocket, 1975; first edition: Paris: Le Livre Contemporain, 1957); *Les bouts de bois de Dieu* (Paris: Presses Pocket, 1971; first edition: Paris: Le Livre Contemporain, 1960); *Voltaïque* (Paris: Présence Africaine, 1962); *L'Harmattan* (Paris: Présence Africaine, 1980; first edition: Paris: Présence Africaine, 1964); *Le mandat, précédé de Véhi-Ciosane* (Paris: Présence Africaine, 1966); *Xala* (Paris: Présence Africaine, 1973); *Le dernier de l'Empire*, Tomes 1 & 2 (Paris: L'Harmattan, 1981); *Niiwam suivi de Taaw* (Paris: Présence Africaine, 1987).

[2] See F. 1. Case, "The Socio-cultural Functions of Women in the Senegalese Novel," *Culture et développement*, 9, 4 (1977): 601-629; also: "Workers' Movements: Revolution and Women's Consciousness in God's Bits of Wood," *Revue canadienne des études africaines / Canadian Journal of African Studies*, 15, 2 (1981): 277-292.

[3] For a discussion of this notion see Arun Mukherjee, *Towards an Aesthetic of Opposition: Essays on Literature, Criticism & Cultural Imperialism* (Ontario: Williams-Wallace, 1988), pp. 10-20.

[4] Bessie Head, *A Question of Power* (London: Heinemann, 1974).

[5] Ngugi wa Thiong'o, *A Grain of Wheat* (London: Heinemann, 1967). Though this and the earlier works of Ngugi were written in English, his later works have been written in Gikuyu and then translated.

[6] Nawal El Saadawi, *The Hidden Face of Eve: Women in the Arab World* (Boston: Beacon, 1980).

[7] Driss Chraibi, *Le passé simple* (Paris: Denoël, 1954).

[8] Assia Djebar, *Les femmes d'Alger dans leur appartement* (Paris: des femmes, 1980).

[9] Chinua Achebe, *Things Fall Apart* (London: Heinemann, 1958).

[10] Sada Niang, "Poétique linguistique de la littérature sénégalaise: Une analyse diachronique" (Unpublished manuscript).

[11] See Case (1981).

[12] For a detailed explanation, see F. 1. Case, "L'Analyse sociocritique du roman africain: problemes d'une methode," in *La lecture sociocritique du texte romanesque*, ed. G. Falconer & H. Mitterand (Toronto: A.M. Hakkert, 1975), pp. 49-62.

[13] *Les bouts de bois de Dieu*, p. 224.

[14] "Taaw," in *Niiwam*, p. 183.

[15] See Nawal El Saadawi, *Memoirs from the Women's Prison* (London: The Women's Press, 1983).

[16] "Taaw," in *Niiwam*, pp. 95-97.

[17] "Lettres de France," in *Voltaïque,* p. 91.

[18] Frantz Fanon, *Les damnés de la terre* (Paris: Maspero, 1968), pp. 79-81.

[19] *Young Cinema and Theatre*, 3 (1970): 27.

[20] From an interview with Sembène in Dakar, Senegal, in 1978.

[21] He was born and partly brought up in rural Casamance and is presently living in Dakar.

[22] From an unpublished interview with Sembène in Atlanta in 1979.

[23] *Ibid.*

[24] *Black Art*, 3, 3 (1979): 33.

[25] From an unpublished interview with Sembène in Dakar in 1978.

[26] From an interview with Sembène conducted by Jean and Ginette Delmas, which appeared in *Jeune cinéma*, 99 (December 1976 - January 1977): 14. (Author's translation.)

[27] D. T. Niane, *Sundiata: An Epic of Old Mali*, transl. G. D. Pickett (London: Longman, 1965), p. 1.

[28] Quoted in Luis H. Francia, "The Other Cinema," *Village Voice*, 17 May 1983, p. 63.

[29] Amadou Hampathé Bâ, *Aspects de la civilisation africaine* (Paris: Présence Africaine, 1972), pp. 22, 26.

[30] Teshome Gabriel, "Third Cinema as Guardian of Popular Memory: Towards a Third Aesthetics," in *Questions of Third Cinema,* ed. Jim Pines and Paul Willemen (London: British Film Institute, 1989), pp. 53-54.

[31] Ibid., p. 54.

[32] Wole Soyinka, *Myth, Literature and the African World* (Cambridge: Cambridge University Press, 1976), p. 99.

[33] Sections of this essay have appeared in my "France's Bureau of Cinema: Financial and Technical Assistance Between 1961 and 1977—Operations and Implications for African Cinema," *Society for Visual Anthropology Review*, 6, 2 (Fall 1990): 80-93.

[34] *Consortium Audiovisuel International* Final Report, 10 May 1979.

[35] Guy Hennebelle, "Entretien avec Jean-René Debrix," *L'Afrique littéraire et artistique*, 43 (1977): 77-89.

[36] Interview with Lucien Patry, Paris, 9 July 1987, in "Francophone African Cinema: French Financial and Technical Assistance 1961 to 1977" by Claire Andrade-Watkins, unpublished dissertation (Boston University, 1989), pp. 20-22.

[37] *Ibid.*, pp. 149-151.

[38] *Ibid.*

[39] Interview with Lucien Gohy, Paris, 16 July 1987, in "Francophone African Cinema" by Andrade-Watkins, p. 156.

[40] Paulin Vieyra, *Le cinéma au Sénégal* (Brussels: Organisation Catholique Internationale du Cinema et du l'Audiovisuel, 1988), p. 38.

[41] *Ibid* ., pp . 164-165 .

[42] "Francophone African Cinema" by Claire Andrade-Watkins, p. 156.

[43] *Ibid.*, p. 157.

[44] *Ibid.*, p. 158.

[45] *Ibid.*

[46] *Ibid.*, p. 159.

[47] *Ibid.*, pp. 160-161.

[48] *Ibid.*, pp. 19-20.

[49] Unpublished interview with Gaston Kabore, Secretary General of FEPACI and Burkinabe filmmaker, November 1989, Washington, D.C.

[50] [The exceptions were Sembène and Ngugi. Ngugi arrived after the others, and when he did, Sembène got up and embraced him heartily, with tears in his eyes—both in joy at seeing someone he had not seen in some time, and in regret that Ngugi remains in exile from his beloved homeland, Kenya. Editors.]

[51] Earl Lovelace, *The Dragon Can't Dance* (Harlow, England: Longman, 1985), pp. 23-24. Reprinted with the permission of the copyright holder, André Deutsch, Limited.

[52] [See Langston Hughes' poem "I, Too." Editors.]

[53] [i.e. the Basilique de Yamoussoukro, constructed in the natal village of President Houphouet-Boigny. Editors.]

BIOGRAPHICAL NOTES
ON CONTRIBUTORS

Claire Andrade-Watkins is a member of the faculty at Emerson College (Boston), where she teaches Film Studies. She is co-editor of *Black Frames: Critical Perspectives on Independent Black Cinema* (1988).

Toni Cade Bambara is a Philadelphia-based free-lance writer, filmmaker, and lecturer with nearly a dozen screenplays, two novels, and several short stories to her credit. Her novel *The Salt Eaters* (1981) won the American Book Award that year, while her film "The Bombing of Osage" earned her the Best Documentary Award from the National Black Programming Consortium in 1986.

Frederick Ivor Case is a professor of French and the current Principal of New College, University of Toronto. Aside from several publications on Sembène's writing, he is the author of numerous articles on Caribbean literature and on Islamic discourse in African literature. Among his more important works are *Racism and National Consciousness* (1979) and *The Crisis of Identity: Studies in the Guadeloupean and Martinican Novel* (1985).

Mbye Cham teaches literature and film at Howard University. He specializes in African and Caribbean film and has co-edited *Black Frames: Critical Perspectives on Independent Black Cinema* (1988). His latest publication is *Ex-iles: Essays on Caribbean Cinema* (1992).

Earl Lovelace is a novelist and playwright who lives and writes in Trinidad, while teaching literature at the University of the West Indies. His novels are *While Gods Are Falling* (1965), *The Schoolmaster* (1968), *The Dragon Can't Dance* (1979), and *The Wine of Astonishment* (1982).

Ngugi wa Thiong'o is one of Africa's best known writers, with six novels to his credit, including *Weep Not Child* (1964), *A Grain of Wheat* (1967), *Petals of Blood* (1977), and *Matigari* (1987). He was detained for a year by the Kenyan government, and since 1982 he has lived in exile. His book of critical essays *Decolonising the Mind: The Politics of Language in African Literature* appeared in 1986. He is professor of Comparative Literature and Performance Studies at New York University.

Sada Niang is assistant professor of African and Caribbean Literature at the University of Victoria, British Columbia. He is the author of numerous articles in internationally known journals, and the co-author of two monographs: *Elsewhere in Africa*, published in Paris by Hatier in 1978, and *African Continuities (L'Héritage africain)*, published by Terebi of Toronto in 1989.

Françoise Pfaff teaches in the Department of Romance Languages at Howard University, Washington, D.C., and is the author of *The Cinema of Ousmane Sembène, A Pioneer of African Film* (1984) and *Twenty-five Black African Filmmakers* (1988).

John Wideman is a novelist who teaches literature at the University of Massachusetts at Amherst. His *Sent for You Yesterday* was awarded the PEN/Faulkner Award for Fiction in 1984. His other novels include *A Glance Away* (1967), *Hurray Home* (1970), *The Lynchers* (1973), *Hiding Place* (1981), and the recent highly acclaimed *Philadelphia Fire: A Novel* (1990).

The Editors: Thomas Cassirer is emeritus professor of French, and Ralph Faulkingham is professor of Anthropology at the University of Massachusetts, Amherst. Samba Gadjigo is associate professor of French at Mount Holyoke College. Formerly associate professor of Black Studies and English at Amherst College, Reinhard Sander now teaches in the Department of Africana Studies at the University of Pittsburgh.

APPENDIX

A Select Bibliography of Ousmane Sembène's Written Works

Le docker noir (Paris: Debresse, 1956). Translated into English by Ros Schwartz and published as *The Black Docker* (London: Heinemann, 1987).

This first work of fiction by Sembène depicts the betrayal suffered by an African writer whose novel is published under false pretenses, and the betrayal suffered by African workers who lead a miserable existence in Marseille. This novel is also a fictional reconstruction of race relations between the French and the exiles from France's colonies in Africa and the black diaspora. Autobiographical in its orientation, it set the political tone for a new breed of works by French-speaking African writers.

O pays, mon beau peuple (Paris: Le Livre Contemporain, 1957).

Sembène's second novel is a lyrical work. Through Oumar Faye's tragic fight for land and freedom for his people, the author explores the issues of race relations, racial intolerance, and mixed marriage in a colonial setting. Sembène focuses on the odyssey of a young Senegalese man who returns from France to the Casamance in southern Senegal with a white wife and the dream to liberate his countrymen and women from colonial exploitation. Oumar's death at the end of this novel points to the tragedy lived daily by colonized people under French rule.

Les bouts de bois de Dieu (Paris: Le Livre Contemporain, 1960). Translated into English by Francis Price and published as *God's Bits of Wood*, with an introduction by A. Adu Boahen (Garden City: Anchor Books, 1970).

By far the most widely read and studied of Sembène's novels, *God's Bits of Wood* is a fictionalized reconstruction of the railroad workers' strike in 1947 that for months paralyzed traffic between Bamako, Thies, and Dakar. A celebration of the people's power and determination to control their own destiny, this work has also been hailed by critics as one of the first African novels to formulate the idea of women as active agents in the historical process of liberating (politically, economically, and culturally) the African continent. Most of all, the novel depicts the different changes that can affect an entire people engaged in a fight to free themselves from foreign exploitation.

Voltaïque (Paris: Présence Africaine, 1962).

With this collection of thirteen stories, Sembène broadens the scope of his artistry. The texts assembled here range from tales ("Mahomoud Fall"), to fables ("Communauté"), short stories ("Devant l'histoire," "Prise de conscience," "La noire de. . .," and "Voltaïque," a story on the origin of tribal scars). The themes in these stories range from the portrayal of African exiles and polygamy to women's power and political consciousness.

L'Harmattan (Paris: Présence Africaine, 1964).

Like *God's Bits of Wood*, this novel is based on historical events that had far-reaching effects on West Africa's political transformation: the 1958 referendum on the future of France's African colonies, organized by General de Gaulle. Set in an unnamed African capital, the story recreates the climate of excitement, hope, fear, and deception experienced by a whole generation of Africans at that time. Through its robust characters, the novel also traces the different political orientations of the intellectual elite on the eve of independence.

Le mandat, précédé de Véhi-Ciosane (Paris: Présence Africaine, 1966). Translated into English by Clive Wake and published as *The Money Order, with White Genesis* (London: Heinemann, 1972).

Adapted into a film as "Mandabi" in 1968, "The Money Order" represents Sembène's first and uncompromising look at the human tragedy of post-colonial Africa. Under the combined effects of an imposed cash economy, an alien administrative system, and illiteracy, the hero Ibrahima Dieng casts a new light on the despair experienced by those left out and forgotten by the empty promises of a corrupt political and economic leadership.

Xala (Paris: Présence Africaine, 1973). Translated into English by Clive Wake and published as *Xala* (Westport: L. Hill and Co., 1976).

Like "The Money Order" this almost farcical novel focuses on contemporary Senegal. Here Sembène uses the image of sexual impotence as a metaphor for the new African comprador bourgeoisie's incompetence, vanity, and inability to lead the newly independent nation. The novel also documents the shocking and widening gap between a self-absorbed wealthy elite class and the multitudes living in extreme poverty.

Le dernier de l'Empire, tomes 1 & 2 (Paris: L'Harmattan, 1981). Translated by Adrian Adams and published as *The Last of the Empire: A Senegalese Novel* (London: Heinemann, 1983).

The context here is by now familiar: nepotism, incompetence, and the abuse of public power rampant in many African states in the decades following independence. Set in independent Senegal, the novel dramatizes the military coup that has been a plague on Africa's political landscape, jeopardizing political stability and economic development.

Niiwam (Paris: Présence Africaine, 1987). Translated into English and published as *Niiwam and Taaw: Two Novellas* (Oxford and Portsmouth, N.H.: Heinemann, 1992).

This work is a collection of two short stories: "Niiwam," which gives the title to the collection, and "Taaw." "Niiwam" tells the story of the peasant Thierno, whose young son Niiwam dies while they are in Dakar. Through Thierno's nightmarish bus trip with his son's body on his knees from the hospital morgue to the Muslim cemetery of Dakar at Yoff, Sembène introduces the reader to the human, material, and moral decay that the fetishism of money has caused in modern urban Africa. As for "Taaw," the dominant theme is the cruel reality of life in suburban Dakar, with its unemployment, poverty, drugs, and lack of moral leadership. We see here as well other themes important to Sembène: generational conflict, teenage pregnancy, and the oppression of women by a culture of patriarchy. But as with many of his other works, "Taaw" ends with a note of rebellion and a hope for a better future for all the oppressed.

Films Written and Directed by Ousmane Sembène

Ousmane Sembène's films are distributed in the United States exclusively by New Yorker Films, 16 West 61st Street, New York, NY 10023, telephone: 212-247-6110. To date, they are available for rent or for purchase in both 16 mm and 32 mm formats, but not on videotape.

"L'EMPIRE SONHRAI"   1963

Sembène's first film is a documentary on the history of the Songhai empire, produced by the government of the Republic of Mali. In French. 16 mm. Black and white. 20 minutes.

"BOROM SARRET"   1963

Spare masterpiece of protest against economic exploitation. Depicts the typical daily encounters of a cart driver in Dakar, Senegal. In French with English sub-titles. 16 mm. Black and white. 20 minutes.

"NIAYE"   1964

Narrated by a village griot, "Niaye" is the tragic tale of a young girl whose pregnancy scandalizes her community. A visiting worker is accused of being responsible for the pregnancy, but subsequently it is discovered that her own father is the culprit. The community strives to keep the scandal from the French colonial administration. In French. 16 mm. Black and white. 35 minutes.

"LA NOIRE DE. . ."   1966

Sembène's first feature film, known in English as "Black Girl," made a profound impression at several international film festivals in 1966. The evolution of the African cinema can probably be dated from this point. Shot in a simple, freewheeling style reminiscent of the early New Wave, it tells a direct, bitter, unambiguous story of exile and despair. The heroine, Diouanna, is a Senegalese maid taken to the Riviera by her French employers. It is only when she is out of Africa that she realizes what being African means: it means being a thing, no longer Diouanna, but "the black girl." Jean Vigo Prize, 1966. In French with English sub-titles. 16 mm. Black and white. 60 minutes.

"MANDABI"   1968

Based on Sembène's short novel *The Money Order*, this feature film is a deceptively simple story of a man who receives a money order from his nephew in Paris and attempts to cash it. "Mandabi" is a deeply moving, witty, masterful portrait of a vain man whose vanity pales against the chicanery and callousness of the youthful ambitious *petite bourgeoisie*. In Wolof with English sub-titles. 16 mm. Color. 90 minutes.

"TAAW"   1970

Taaw is a young unemployed man in modern Senegal who fends off accusations of laziness for his unemployment and makes a home for his pregnant girlfriend who has been rejected by her family. In Wolof with English sub-titles. 16 mm. Color. 24 minutes.

"EMITAÏ"   1971

"Emitaï" is a historical film that functions also as a timeless allegory. In his clear, spare style, Sembène depicts the clash between French colonists and the Diola of Senegal in the closing days of World War II. It is the women who provide the first voice of resistance and the film conveys their social power as the retainers of ancient myths, rituals, and recent history. In Diola and French with English sub-titles. 16 mm. Color. 101 minutes.

"XALA" 1974

Sembène's savage and hilarious satire of the modern African bourgeoisie was heavily censored in Senegal. Forsaking the more obvious (and politically acceptable) targets of European exploitation and racism, Sembène here zeroes in on a far touchier subject: the entire blackfacing of white colonial policies after independence was granted. The hero of the film is a self-satisfied, westernized Senegalese businessman who is suddenly struck down with the *xala*, an ancient Senegalese curse rendering him impotent. His vain search for a cure becomes a metaphor for the impossibility of Africans achieving liberation through dependence on western technology and bureaucratic structures. In French with English sub-titles. 16 mm. Color. 123 minutes.

"CEDDO"   1976

An exciting political thriller concerning the kidnapping of a beautiful princess is used to examine the confrontation between opposing forces in the face of Muslim expansion. The *ceddo*, or commoner class, refuse to submit to Islam. Set loosely in the 19th century, "Ceddo" is not strictly a historical film, as it ranges far and wide to include philosophy, fantasy, militant politics, and a couple of electrifying leaps across the centuries. In Wolof with English sub-titles. 16 mm. Color. 120 minutes.

"CAMP DE THIAROYE"   1989

Towards the end of 1944, at a bleak military transit camp in Senegal, soldiers from several parts of Africa who have fought with the Free French army to overthrow fascism in Europe, await demobilization, severance pay, and a trip home. French Captain Raymond sincerely tries to convince his Senegalese NCO Diatta that the massacres by French troops, such as that in which Diatta's parents were killed, are a banished phenomenon from the Vichy past. The film's dialectic is intent on proving him wrong. By the end, Raymond has been ostracized as a Communist by his fellow officers, and gradually the attempt by the French command to cheat the African veterans out of their severance pay provokes a mutiny. The French response is an armored attack on the camp with a near total loss of life. "Camp de Thiaroye" is true both to the historical record of

the massacre and to the underlying culture of European imperialism. In Wolof
and French with English sub-titles. Color. 153 minutes.

"GELWAAR"   1992

In choosing "Gelwaar: An African Legend for the 21st Century" for the opening
of the 13th Pan-African Film Festival (in Ouagadougou, Burkina Faso, February
1993), the organizers of this event sought to honor Ousmane Sembène as the
father of African cinema. "Gelwaar" is based on a true story: The body of Pierre
Henri Thioune, alias Gelwaar and leader of a Christian community, is mistakenly
delivered to Muslims who bury him in a Muslim cemetery following the
teachings of Islam. When the mistake is found out, the Christians seek to recover
"their" body. Sembène in this film develops familiar themes: real versus
imaginary independence, women's emancipation, the brain drain to the West,
and dependency on foreign aid. In Wolof and French with English sub-titles.
Color. 115 minutes.

A Critical Bibliography on Ousmane Sembène's Works

Aje, S. O. "L'Importance de l'écriture en tant qu'institution sociale dans *L'Argent* (Emile Zola), *Le roi des Aulnes* (Michel Tournier) et *Le mandat* (Ousmane Sembène)." *Neohelicon*, 16, 1 (1989): 237-255.

Akpadomonye, Patrick. "La parodie et la re-écriture chez Sembène Ousmane: Problèmes textologiques." *Neohelicon*, 16, 2 (1989): 211-219.

Anyidoho, Kofi. "African Creative Fiction and a Poetics of Social Change." *Komparatistische-Hefte*, 13 (1986): 67-81.

Bayo, Ogunjimi. "Ritual Archetypes: Ousmane's Aesthetic Medium in 'Xala.'" *Ufahamu*, 14, 3 (1985): 128-138.

Berrian, Brenda. "Through Her Prism of Social and Political Contexts: Sembène's Female Characters in 'Tribal Scars.'" In *Ngambika: Studies of Women in African Literature*, ed. Carole Boyce Davies and Anne Adams Graves. Trenton, NJ: Africa World Press, 1986. Pp. 195-204.

Cancel, Robert. "Epic Element in 'Ceddo.'" *Current Bibliography on African Affairs*, 18, 1 (1985-1986): 3-19.

Case, F. "Workers' Movements: Revolution and Women's Consciousness in *God's Bits of Wood*." *Canadian Journal of African Studies/Revue canadienne des études africaines*, 15, 2 (1981): 277-292.

Cham, Mbye Baboucar. "Ousmane Sembène and the Aesthetics of African Oral Traditions." *Africana Journal*, 13, 1-4 (1982): 24-40.

Cham, Mbye Baboucar. "Art and Ideology in the Work of Sembène Ousmane and Haile Gerima." *Présence africaine*, 129, 1 (1984): 79-91.

Cnockaert, André. "Véhi-Ciosane, recit clé dans l'oeuvre de Sembène Ousmane." *Zaire-Afrique*, 28, 222 (1988): 109-121.

Feuser, Willfried F. "Richard Wright's Native Son and Ousmane Sembène's *Le docker noir*." *Komparatistische-Hefte*, 14 (1986): 103-116.

Gabriel, Teshone H. "'Xala': A Cinema of Wax and Gold." *Présence africaine*, 116 (1980): 202-214.

Harrow, Kenneth W. "Art and Ideology in *Les bouts de bois de Dieu*: Realism's Artifices." *The French Review*, 62, 3 (February 1989): 483-493.

Harrow, Kenneth "Sembène Ousmane's 'Xala': The Use of Film and Novel as Revolutionary Weapon." *Studies in Twentieth Century Literature*, 4, 2 (Spring 1980): 177-188.

Huannou, Adrien. "L'Islam et le christianisme face à la domination coloniale dans *Les bouts de bois de Dieu*." *Nouvelles du Sud*, 6 (1986-1987): 41-48.

Iyam, David Uru. "The Silent Revolutionaries: Ousmane Sembène's 'Emitai,' 'Xala,' and 'Ceddo.'" *African Studies Review*, 29, 4 (December 1986): 79-87.

Linkhorn, Renée. "L'Afrique de demain: Femmes en marche dans l'oeuvre de Sembène Ousmane." *Modern Language Studies*, 16, 3 (Summer 1986): 69-76.

Lüsebrink, Hans-Jürgen. "De l'incontournabilité de la fiction dans la connaissance historique: questionnements théoretiques à partir de romans historiques contemporains de Alejo Carpentier, de Yambo Ouologuem et d'Ousmane Sembène." *Neohelicon*, 16, 2 (1989): 107-128.

Makolo, Muswaswa. "La solidarité africaine hier, aujourd'hui et demain, dans *Le mandat* de Sembène Ousmane." *Zaire-Afrique*, 145 (1980): 289-300.

Makward, Edris. "Women, Tradition, and Religion in Sembène Ousmane's Work." In *Faces of Islam in African Literature*, ed. Kenneth W. Harrow. Portsmouth, NH: Heinemann, 1991. Pp. 187-199.

Maxwell, Richard. "The Reality Effect of Third World Cinema: Ethnography in 'Ceddo' and 'Ramparts of Clay.'" *Cresset*, 43, 3 (January 1980): 21-22.

Mortimer, Mildred. *Journeys Through the French African Novel*. Portsmouth, NH: Heinemann, 1990. Pp. 69-103.

Mpoyi-Buatu, Th. "'Ceddo' de Sembène Ousmane et 'West Indies' de Med Hondo." *Présence africaine*, 119 (1981): 152-164.

Mzamane, M. V. "Three Novelists of the African Revolution." *Heritage*, 3, (1979): 54-57.

Ojo, S. Ade. "Revolt, Violence and Duty in Ousmane Sembène's *God's Bits of Wood*." *Nigeria Magazine*, 53, 3 (July - September 1985): 58-68.

Peters, Jonathan A. "Sembène Ousmane as Griot: *The Money Order with White Genesis*." *African Literature Today*, 12 (1982): 88-103.

Peters, Jonathan A. "Aesthetics and Ideology in African Film: Ousmane Sembène's

'Emitai.'" In *African Literature in Its Social and Political Dimensions*, ed. Eileen Julien, Mildred Mortimer, and Curtis Schade. Washington: Three Continents Press, 1986. Pp. 69-75.

Pfaff, Françoise. "Myths, Traditions, and Colonialism in Ousmane Sembène's 'Emitai.'" *College Language Association Journal*, 24, 3 (March 1981): 336-346.

Pfaff, Françoise. *The Cinema of Ousmane Sembène, A Pioneer of African Film*. Westport, Connecticut: Greenwood Press, 1984.

Scharfman, Ronnie. "Fonction romanesque feminine: Rencontre de la culture et de la structure dans *Les bouts de bois de Dieu*." *Ethiopiques* 1, 3-4 (1983): 134-144.

Tenaille, Frank and Charles Lemaire. "Samory Touré à l'écran." *Nouvelle Afrique*, 1939 (September 17, 1986): 18-19.

Tine, Alioune. "Wolof ou français, le choix de Sembène." *Notre librairie*, 81 (1985): 43-50.

Vieyra, Paulin. *Ousmane Sembène Cinéaste*. Paris: Présence Africaine, 1973.

Zell, Hans M. *A New Reader's Guide to African Literature*. New York: Africana Publishing Company, 1983. (Note: Zell lists Sembène's entry under "Ousmane.")